THE PREADOLESCENT

A HANDBOOK OF MIDDLE SCHOOL CLASSROOM STRATEGIES

Mary Prentice
Edna Yancey

illustrated by Judith Bynum

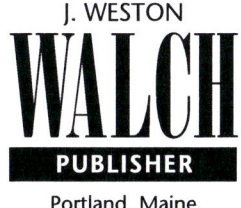

Portland, Maine

The Preadolescent: A Handbook of Middle School Classroom Strategies

This work is dedicated to you, the teachers at the middle school level. The ideas presented in this book came from you and are offered here to be shared with others of our profession.

We would like to express our deepest appreciation to Drs. Gloria Frasier, Jerry Flack, and Annie Calkins. Somehow they managed to find the time to review and offer suggestions. We would like to thank the administrators and teachers who field-tested and developed the various units in the text.

Of course, it was the middle school students who became our "master teachers."

For the next generation with respect and love:

Richard and Prentice,

Jessica and Kent,

Paige and Morgan.

User's Guide to *Walch Reproducible Books*

As part of our general effort to provide educational materials which are as practical and economical as possible, we have designated this publication a "reproducible book." The designation means that the purchase of the book includes purchase of the right to limited reproduction of all pages on which this symbol appears:

Here is the basic Walch policy: We grant to individual purchasers of this book the right to make sufficient copies of reproducible pages for use by all students of a single teacher. This permission is limited to a single teacher, and does not apply to entire schools or school systems, so institutions purchasing the book should pass the permission on to a single teacher. Copying of the book or its parts for resale is prohibited.

Any questions regarding this policy or request to purchase further reproduction rights should be addressed to:

Permissions Editor
J. Weston Walch, Publisher
321 Valley Street • P.O. Box 658
Portland, Maine 04104-0658

Cover illustration by José Ortega

1 2 3 4 5 6 7 8 9 10

ISBN 0-8251-3267-3

Copyright © 1997

J. Weston Walch, Publisher

P. O. Box 658 • Portland, Maine 04104-0658

Printed in the United States of America

Contents

Introduction to Model

Focusing the Various Perspectives 2

Portrait of a Preadolescent 3

Change Personified 5

The Processing Styles of the Human Brain 10

MIA-ADC (Motivate, Integrate, Associate/Activate,
    Demonstrate, Communicate) 18

Introduction to Units

Curriculum Development Process 24

Map It! Learn It! Keep It! 25
    Judith Bynum

Eat a Dandelion 35
    Tammie Tripp-Dillion

Architecture: The Structure of Our Lives 48
    Judith Bynum

Welcome to My World 57
    Kathleen Mariko Yanamura

The Great Depression 69
    Judith Bynum

Change 80
    Helen Hughes, Cindy Middleton, and Edna Yancey

Introduction to Model

Focusing the Various Perspectives

One of the greatest assets of today's American public educational system is the diversity of its teachers. We come from different institutions of training, with different levels of experience in various subject areas. We share a common vision: "To prepare today's students for full participation in tomorrow's world." Each of us strives in our own way to meet the needs of students. Because of our varied experiences and perspectives, the opportunities for American students to participate in a superior educational experience are vast. At the same time, this very diversity may create stumbling blocks when trying to organize a framework through which students' needs will be met during the middle school years.

The greatest asset—in this case teacher diversity—has the potential to become a liability. Without excellent rapport, misunderstandings and misconceptions may impede progress. Working on committees, we may become exasperated, frustrated, or bewildered as we attempt to achieve common goals. At one time or another, most of us fall into the trap of using jargon or specialized vocabulary, with the assumption that everyone understands exactly what *we* mean with *our* terminology.

The purpose of this book is to provide the focus essential for a middle or junior high school team approach. It provides a common vocabulary, allowing diversity to become a strength and a framework to achieve common goals.

This book is based on four assumptions:

1. We, as educators, need to understand the vast changes that occur during the preadolescent age span.

2. To benefit students, we need to apply recent research on the brain in our teaching practices.

3. We must share a common awareness of the importance of integrating teams and/or themes for the students' sake.

4. We must must support the use of a theme and/or team concept to provide the most effective instruction and services for students.

The book offers:

1. Characteristics of the preadolescent age group

2. An overview of how the brain functions

3. A model developed by teachers and for teachers that allows individuals to function comfortably and effectively in teams, regardless of prior training, cultural differences, or educational background

4. Applications of the model utilizing middle school units

5. Full-page illustrations, which you may wish to copy and distribute to students in your classes

Every one of us in the teaching profession has countless demands on our time and energy. When we learn to support one another effectively by working in teams or with integrated themes of curriculum, we will not only benefit our students, but also ourselves.

Portrait of a Preadolescent

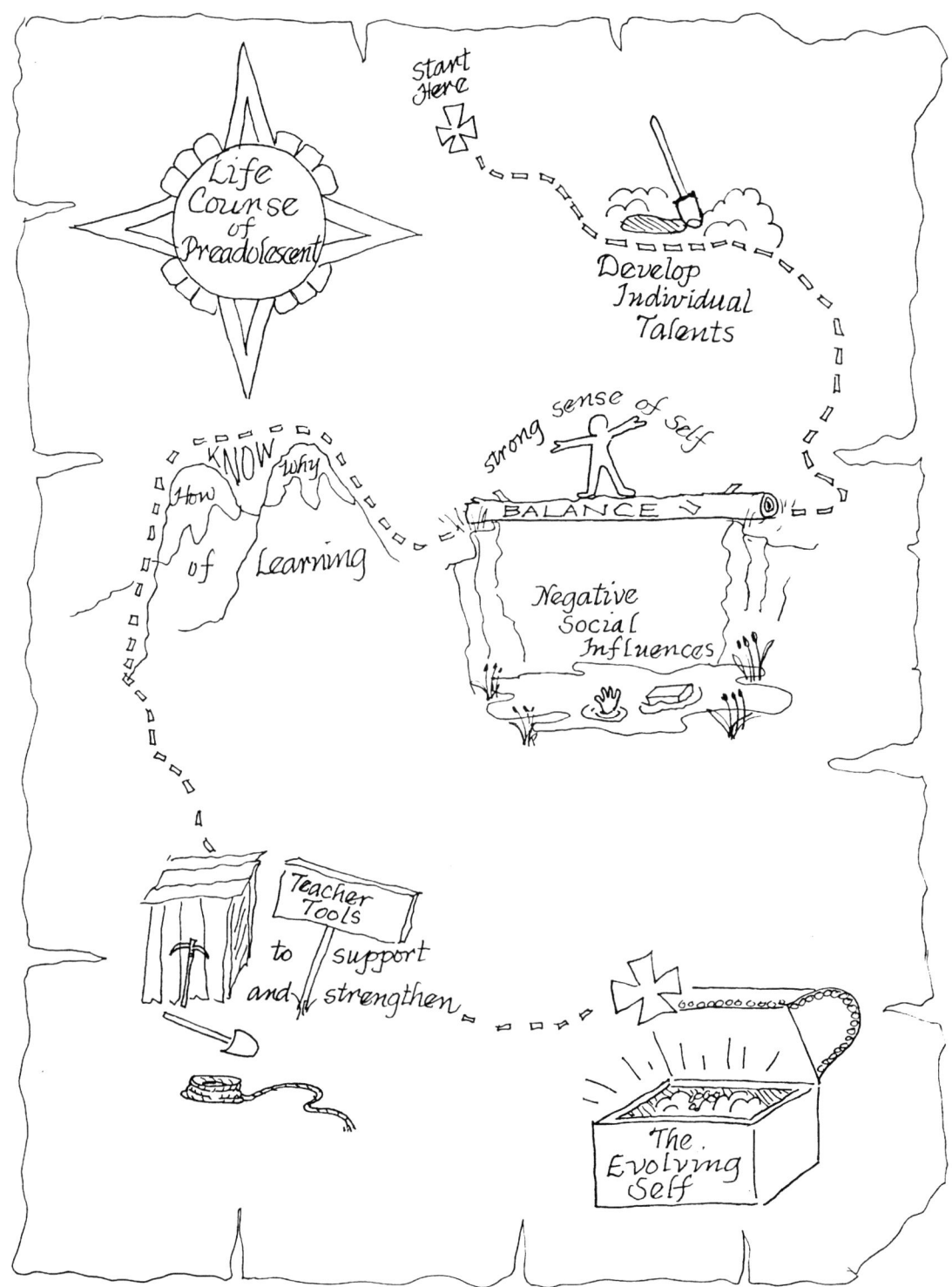

Portrait of A Preadolescent

Elizabeth is alive—in the truest sense of the word. She vibrates with energy and excitement. She typically chatters, rather than talks. Her words come at a rate faster than that of a dot matrix printer. She doesn't think and then speak. She speaks and discovers from the sound of her own voice what she feels, who she is, and what she knows.

Elizabeth will play baseball or fight with the best of them. She cannot spell patience, and this may be because she is not on speaking terms with the concept. There was no yesterday, and tomorrow is only a vague adult world. There is for her only a vigorous, powerfully consuming NOW.

She hears, but rarely listens. She comprehends at a level that is far above what is said, implied, or read. She takes in the world, not through her five senses, but through every power and nerve of her being. At times her happiness trails her like the tail of a comet, but it never catches her or possesses her for long. She assumes it, but never examines it.

From all appearances, Elizabeth operates not on a logical, moral realm, but from an intuitive force. She just *knows*. She knows how far she can push you before you explode. She knows how to get her own way most of the time. She knows how to make her father jump hoops gladly. She knows how to intimidate, inspire, and frustrate others. She does all of these things equally well.

Yesterday I watched her touch, hug, and freely express her caring to others with complete naturalness. At long last, I knew I had some real insight into, and understanding of, my young student and friend Elizabeth.

Today, she came into the classroom without a word. She walked, as a mule straining at the weight of a plow, straight to her desk. She spoke to no one. While others enjoyed the give and take of a new day, she refused to partake. She stared at me in a remote, almost defiant way. She dared us all to enter her space or attempt to populate her world. Her eyes would go over the page, but there was no spirit for the silent concepts to communicate with. She was lost in her feelings. The pain of being had cramped her into an immovable stance. Today, she would be a spectator of the world. Perhaps tomorrow she would again be a participant. But not today.

Elizabeth is predictably unpredictable. Inconsistency rules her personality. Trance is her shadow, incompleteness her constant companion. What a challenge to be her teacher! As I watch this emerging individual explore her worlds in search of self, I know she will find it many times. But for now, this preadolescent is caught in the middle, neither child nor adult, but clearly an evolving individual struggling to define herself. This time I get to watch.

Change Personfied

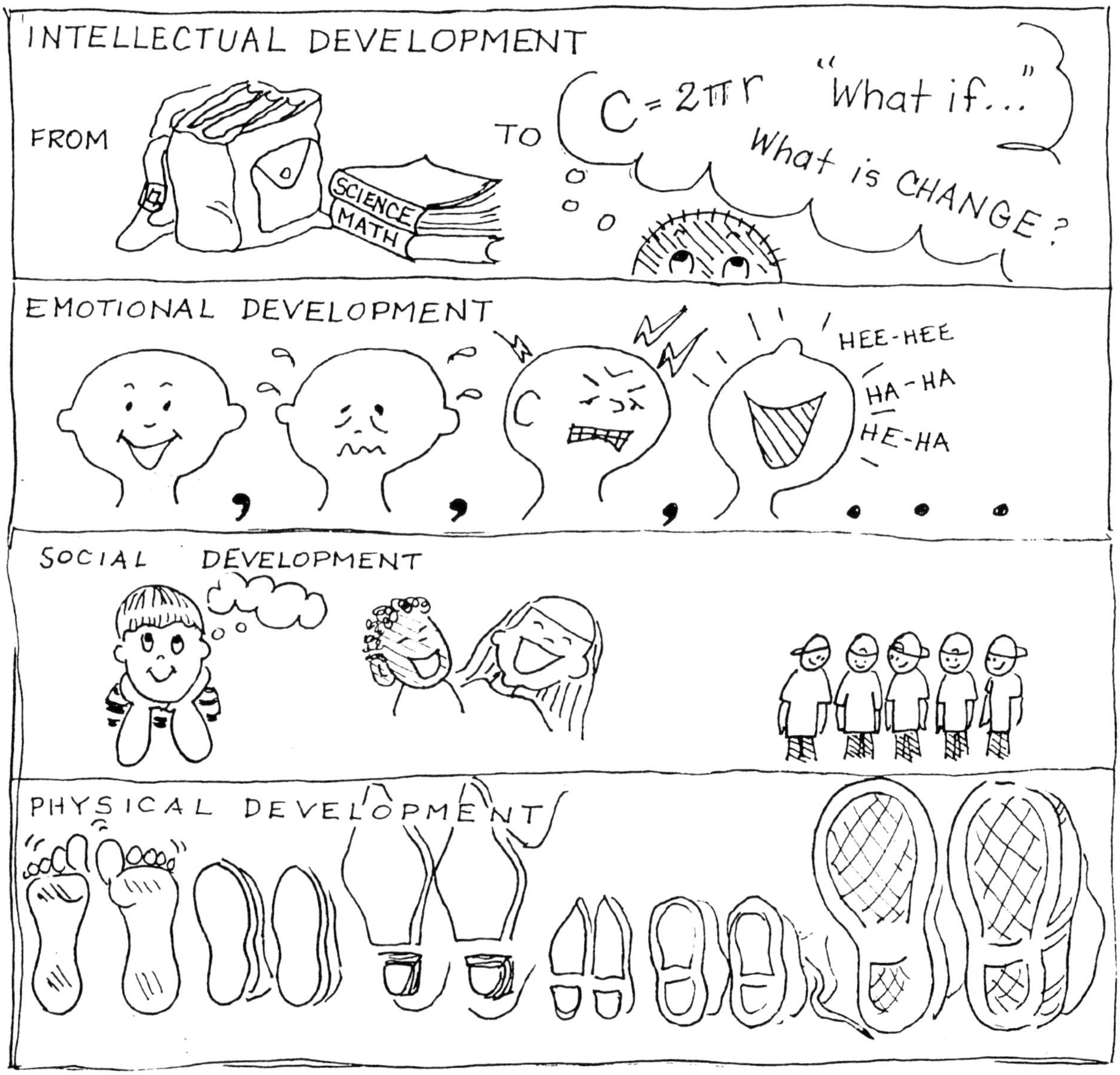

... in the process of

becoming

Change Personified

Stress and storm are its core. Ambivalence is its indicator. It is a time of vast changes. Although the dynamic preadolescent nature is familiar to all of us working with these challenging youth, the 1990's resurgence of the middle school movement has created an interest in reexamining their different characteristics and needs. The preadolescent years are indeed a fascinating metamorphic vortex in every developmental area: intellectual, emotional, social, and physical.

Intellectual Development

or
Where does a trout go when it's raining?

One of the most dramatic changes that occurs during preadolescence is in the cognitive arena. According to Beane and Lipka (1984), "While the child has been limited to thinking about concrete relationships between concepts and ideas, the transescent begins to develop a capacity for abstract or conceptual thought" (p. 22). This qualitative transition allows for the development of an ability to build or understand ideas, abstract theories, or concepts without any regard to whether they have been previously experienced. "What if" questions abound, and futuristic thinking begins to surface.

With this newly formed cognitive leap, life becomes exciting. Yet, without a strong sense of self, it is also confusing, intriguing, and sometimes frightening. Many preadolescents become caught between the world that is familiar to them and the world that is unknown. They are still not able to leave the concrete world behind, but they are not comfortable entering the world of abstract thoughts and ideas either. Going from the known into the unknown becomes a difficult process. Thus, we can expect periods of vacillation between fact and fantasy. Every one of us at this level has been asked unfathomable questions such as, "Where does a trout go when it's raining?" We need to exercise patience with unexpected thought patterns and gentle guidance to step-by-step logical conclusions.

Emotional Development

or
If David calls me that name again,
Mr. Howard, I'll hit him! I don't
care what you say!
Can I PLEASE hit him?

The preadolescent is immersed in a search for a unique identity, which requires an exploration within and without. There is a tremendous need to protect this evolving identity at any cost, which may lead to extreme mood swings and a continuum of diverse overt behaviors. Alexander, et al. (1969) describes the flux of behavior changes: contented and amiable one moment; aggressive, belligerent, and argumentative the next moment. Extreme sensitivity allows feelings to be hurt easily. The anger and hurt of the preadolescent is more intense and deeper than that of younger children; often there is a desire to strike out with more fervor.

All of us working with this age group know that preadolescents are frequently impulsive and ambivalent. They are often anxious, doubtful, and confused. Altercations break out spontaneously and sometimes are very painfully and slowly resolved. It is extremely easy for us to become caught up in the preadolescent's emotional intensity. It is of critical importance, though, that we maintain adult objectivity, so that opportunities of acting as a positive role model are not missed. How else might preadolescents learn how to deal effectively with anger, rejection, or belittlement?

Social Development

or
I know I passed the note to Dana, Mrs. Davis!
You moved her to the other side of the room.
I don't have anyone to talk to over here!
PLEASE don't read the note!

The emergence of peer-group influence over parental influence marks the major social change for the preadolescent. This is the stage in which they transfer their security base from home and parents to peers. Early adolescents view their friendships as intimate and regard loyalty or faithfulness as critical factors for maintaining desired closeness (Berndt, et al., 1990).

Even though the movement is away from parental influence, the preadolescent still desires to relate and identify with adults other than parents. This affords us an ideal opportunity to influence students with insights into self and interactions with others by modeling appropriate social skills and conduct.

Physical Development

or

*Ms. Wiles, did you know Mike
keeps a condominium in his wallet?*

Two major biological events occur during this period: Boys often catch up to and surpass girls in height and weight; and menarche takes place in the majority of girls. Inquisitiveness about their changing bodies is a focal point for preadolescents during this developmental period. Sex becomes a major issue which can become fraught with misconceptions due to inadequate information. Our ability to correct possible fallacies may be diminished because preadolescents often think their peers "know more." It is important that we openly and honestly answer any troubling questions that might arise, because the occasions to do so may be very brief and only sporadic. Also, we must be careful not to forget that in terms of gender, boys and girls are vastly different and often require different approaches.

Summary

Preadolescents—they are alike but different, consistent in their inconsistencies, constantly changing and always challenging. They are neither this nor that, but in the process of "becoming." Because of their vulnerability, they desire and deserve teachers who not only support, but who also understand and accept them. Most importantly, they need instructors who are willing to create student-centered classrooms specifically designed for this time of personal turmoil. Based on the latest scientific and medical research, the MIA-ADC model (Prentice, 1994) will assist teachers in this vital effort by reflecting the brain's ability to detect and store information. The following chapters introduce the model and its application.

References

Alexander, W.M., et al. *The Emergent Middle School.* New York: Holt, Rinehart, and Winston, Inc., 1969.

Beane, J.A., and R.P. Lipka. *Self-Concept, Self-Esteem, and the Curriculum.* Newton, MA: Allyn and Bacon, Inc., 1984.

Berndt, T.J., et al. "Friends' Influence on Adolescents' Academic Achievement Motivation: An Experimental Study." *Journal of Educational Psychology,* 1990, 82, pp. 664–670.

Prentice, M. *Catch Them Learning: A Handbook of Classroom Strategies.* Palatine, IL: IRI/Skylight Publishing, Inc., 1994.

The Processing Styles of the Human Brain

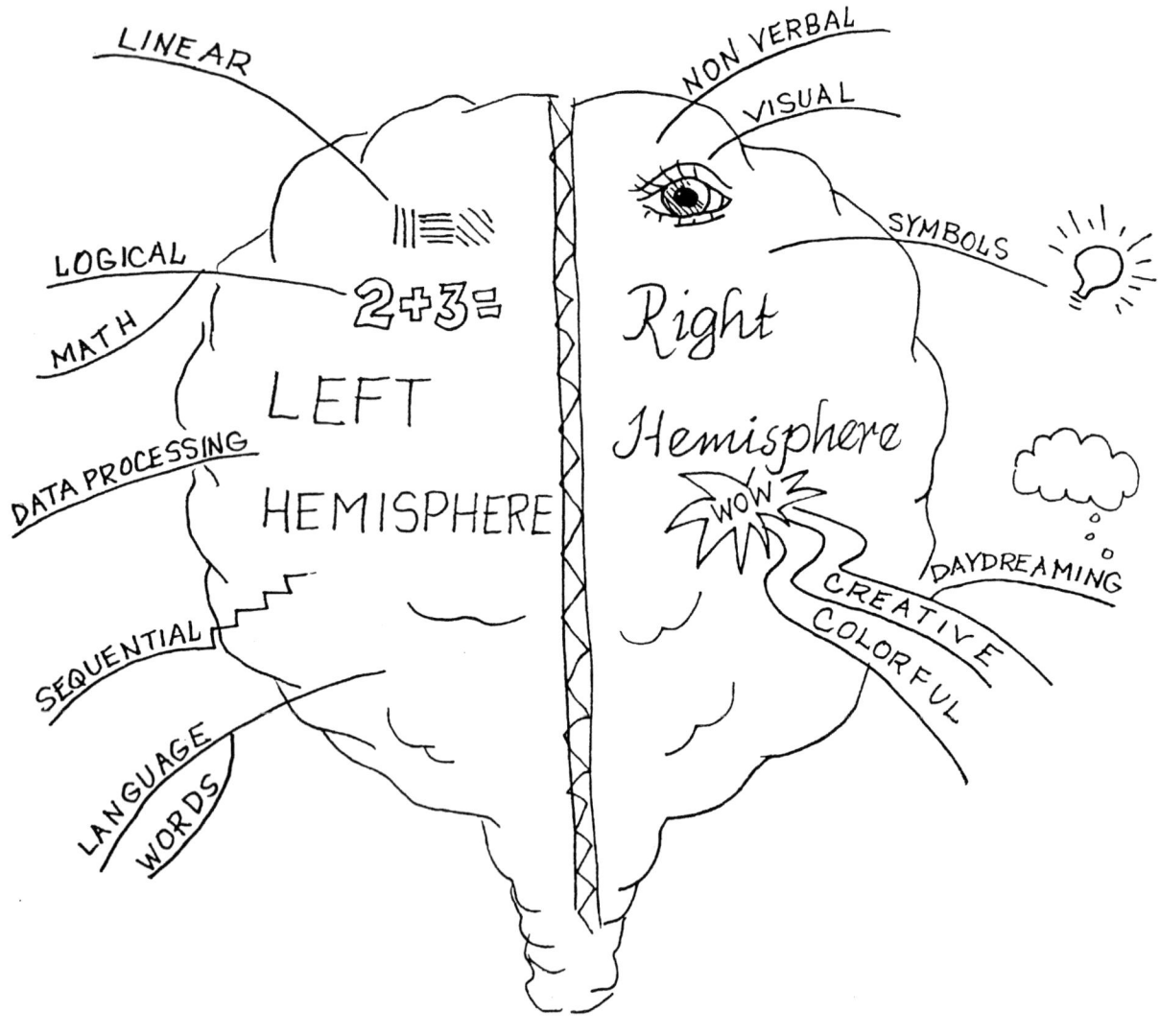

The Processing Styles of the Human Brain

The brain is a pattern detector. That's its job. In fact, the brain is designed to recognize, detect, and construct patterns. The brain detects patterns by the clues we feed it. These clues come to us either through our genes or through our experiences. We enter the world with preprogrammed genes, but our senses encode and imprint our experiences from birth on. A basic assumption of this book is that if we as educators grasp how the brain functions, we can help students learn to use their minds more effectively.

In recent years, the medical profession has offered new insights into how the brain functions. While the brain is still largely a mystery, we do know that it is a multipath, complex, multimodal, functioning organ. The brain programs whatever messages we send to ourselves through our senses. It programs electronically and chemically. These programs are imprinted and recorded. What the brain is told, it accepts uncensored and unconditionally.  This innate search for meaning occurs through our unique brain patterning; thus, each of us learns in a highly personalized, individualized fashion.

Today's students are often bombarded with negative perceptions from real life, as well as from the fiction of TV. For example, instant gratification is often portrayed as reality. Without appropriate patterns to provide alternative perspectives for these images, students may have confused perceptions and limited choices. If they are not aware of alternatives, they may not be capable of discerning the positive in themselves, others, or the world. It is imperative that we provide students with experiences and choices that encourage them to identify and bring to the conscious level the positive attributes of themselves and others. To accomplish this, we must examine three major issues:

1. What is presently known about how the brain function

2. How the concept of intelligence is changing

3. The impact of specific changes of preadolescence in the cognitive, affective, social, and physical domains

At one time, intelligence was conceptualized as a one-factor, single, measurable entity, and educators designed teaching to fit this conception. Teachers provided the facts; students memorized and mastered. We pronounced them educated as they mastered a certain standard of factual information. This approach paralleled the agronomy stage of our culture. Students of that period learned from the past; parents and grandparents taught them the when, where, and how-to of an agricultural economy.

As the industrial stage emerged, and women were initially drawn from the home to the workplace, the production line became the focus and measure of success. IQ tests were widely administered as a standardized measurement of ability. Educators during this stage shifted their emphasis for learning from the past to the present. While a higher percentage of the population attended schools, not all members were afforded equal access to equal educational opportunities. As a nation we took pride in the fact that a higher percentage of our youth was enrolled for longer periods of time. The assembly line was often a fit metaphor for the educational system at this stage of our nation's development.

With the advent of technology came the knowledge base explosion. John Naisbitt, author of *Megatrends* (1991), suggests that the knowledge base may soon double in days, not decades. Educators of today are preparing students for a future we cannot fully conceptualize and only dimly imagine. Yet many schools of today are still patterned on the production-line model, where one style of learning fits all, even though just knowing the facts is no longer enough. What today's students must know is **how to learn**, and **the value of learning**. Students must be able to use their minds well if they are to achieve their future dreams in the twenty-first century. Fogarty (1994) echoes this philosophy when she states:

> *The skillful teacher teaches not only for the moment, but for the long run. The superior teacher naturally causes students to be aware of their own learning and to be strategic and reflective about that learning. This thoughtful student reflection, in turn, fosters creative application and transfer of ideas as students bridge learning into their everyday lives (p. xix).*

In summary, the shift has been from an agricultural society to a manufacturing society to an information-based society. Current literature seems to indicate that we are now moving from an information-based society to a communication-based society. This societal shift, together with the shift from a physical occupation emphasis to a focus on "mind work" employment, means one can no longer depend on earning a living in the local store. Students of the twenty-first century must be prepared to compete within the context of a global economy.

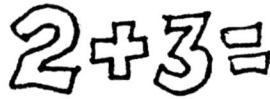

The movement of society toward a more abstract means of earning a living demands a new mind-set for the preadolescent of this generation. Today's students must appreciate the value of learning as a process in order to obtain their place in the future. This shift in emphasis away from learning characterized by rote memorization of facts has become so critical that in 1994, Congress passed goals for the year 2000. These goals demand that *all* children will start school ready to learn. Every school in America will ensure that all students learn to use their minds well so that they will be prepared for responsible citizenship, further learning, and productive employment.

The Goals 2000: Educate America Act establishes the national goals and standards. The Improving America's Schools Act of 1994 focuses on changes within the elementary and secondary education level, as well as changes in the Title 1 program. The School-to-Work Opportunities Act of 1993 links academic and work-based learning. Each contains information directly affecting the task and focus of educators.

Additional new insights on brain functioning from the medical field, coupled with the broadened view of a spectrum of intelligence from educators, have initiated and intensified scholarly research on intelligence. Several outstanding theories have been presented. Two of these are Howard Gardner's multiple intelligences and Robert Sternberg's triarchic theory of human intelligence. For the purpose of this work, Gardner's theory is fundamental. To bridge the gap between theory and the classroom, there are several excellent works that educators could examine. For example, Carolyn Chapman, in *If the Shoe Fits...: How to Develop Multiple Intelligences in the Classroom* (1993), provides hundreds of techniques and strategies for facilitating the development of multiple intelligences in the classroom. Chapman incorporates the intent of Gardner's theory by selecting only those practical instructional tools that usefully translate the theory into practice. David Lazear's *Seven Ways of Knowing* (1991) and *Seven Ways of Teaching* (1992) and 1994 publication of the Association for Supervision and Curriculum Development, *Multiple Intelligences in the Classroom,* by Thomas Armstrong, are other excellent sources. Armstrong provides examples of ways to incorporate the multiple intelligences into curriculum development, encompassing areas such as thematic instruction, special education, and computer technology.

The basic premise of rethinking curriculum is to provide teachers with skills that make learning more accessible for all students, because it is compatible with the ways their individual brains function.

According to Caine and Caine (1991), "Learning is a physiological process. The physical structure of the brain changes as a result of experience"(p. 27).

Once we accept these concepts, we use a variety of learning styles in curricular activities—auditory, visual, and kinesthetic—to help students relate to real-world experiences.

Unfortunately, many adults relate to students from their preferred learning styles, unless they become aware of the benefits of presenting curriculum in a multimodel fashion.

Many teachers in America have received no training in the importance, value, and necessity of presenting information in a way that is compatible with students' varied learning styles.

Preadolescents do attempt to tell us their preferred modalities. If we are astute, we can discern the preferred modality by observing, listening, and interacting with their students. For example, kinesthetic learners tend to learn by doing. They enjoy action. As they describe what happened, they tend to use body movement and gesturing. They do not like to plan, and they typically attack tasks step-by-step.

Visual learners tend to learn by observing. They enjoy reading and describing the way things look. They exhibit a myriad of facial expressions. They tend to like to plan in advance, organize, and create lists.

Auditory learners tend to learn by listening. They enjoy music and talking. They describe things in terms of sounds. Educators gain insight into the auditory learner when they listen to the student's tone of voice. These students love to talk about things, and through talking they often come to an understanding of the topic.

We can very readily identify types of learners by simply presenting a lesson to the class and categorizing the responses over a period of time. For example, kinesthetic learners often will respond with "I got it," visual learners with "I see what you mean," and auditory learners with "I hear you." However, we should bear in mind that one such response does not make a pattern.

Effective learning occurs when relationships are made across the disciplines. According to Caine & Caine (1991), thematic teaching and other methods of integration of the curriculum are only two approaches to learning, but they orchestrate complex experiences in a way that takes advantage of what the brain does well.

Although we may understand the benefits of workng in teams, many of us may have had little or no training in the strategies and skills needed to be effective team members. Teamwork becomes further complicated because we have received training at different institutions in different subject areas. We use different vocabularies or mind-sets to address issues associated with a task.

The MIA-ADC model (Prentice, 1994) proposed here was developed after examining several strategies for writing curriculum from various subject domains. It contains major constructs common to all and is therefore teacher friendly and quickly mastered. The model is particularly beneficial in light of recent inclusion strategies that have been widely embraced in the classroom at every level, as it is supportive of this concept.

The MIA-ADC model requires a fundamental shift in perspectives, not a recycling of terminology. It is supported by the medical and scientific community and by significant facts about how the brain detects and stores information. The model presupposes that we will be more effective if the preadolescent is actively engaged in a learning process designed to accommodate the science of the brain and its ability to process information.

The model assists us no matter what level of teaching expertise we possess. The model is compatible with those teaching specific subject domains from various educational backgrounds. The essentials leading to successful team writing for maximum student learning are:

1. **Motivate:** Engage students in the learning process.

2. **Integrate:** Determine which subjects and/or contexts are most appropriate for a specific topic or theme.

3. **Associate:** Choose the grouping pattern that is best for this specific instructional goal.

4. **Activate:** Help students become engaged in a subject so that they can master its content.

5. **Demonstrate:** Explain the types of assessment used to demonstrate learning.

6. **Communicate:** Allow students to fully share, so that they can experience the benefits of learning and working together.

Summary

Never before have we been besieged by so many needs and demands, or so vast a range of changes requiring our immediate attention. Society shares one common denominator—our schools. It is within these walls that tomorrow's adults are learning how to learn, and their enthusiasm for learning will be the compass that leads them into the twenty-first century. As we come to appreciate how the brain functions, the benefits of helping students to accept, appreciate, and focus on developing their individual talents is self-evident. A strong sense of self is critical to counterbalancing the sometimes negative and detrimental social influences, so prevalent in the contemporary social environment. Preadolescents often experience the vacillation of extremes in every aspect of their lives: intellectual, emotional, social, and physical.

The preadolescent period affords teachers and parents an unparalleled opportunity for strengthening the learning process. Using the evidence of brain research and the broadening perspectives of intelligence, MIA-ADC lays a foundation for us to respond to the needs of preadolescents. The adequacy of the response becomes a critical issue for all of the support systems involved with preadolescents. For it is at this age that individuals most often chart their life course. They may become masters at playing the game of self-denial, or they may gain insights that support and strengthen their evolving selves.

References

Armstrong, T. *Multiple Intelligences in the Classroom.* Alexandria, VA: Association for Supervision and Curriculum Development, 1994.

Caine, R.N, and G. Caine. *Making Connections: Teaching and the Human Brain.* Alexandria, VA: Association for Supervision and Curriculum Development, 1991.

Chapman, C. *If the Shoe Fits...: How to Develop Multiple Intelligences in the Classroom.* Palatine, IL: IRI/Skylight Publishing, 1991.

Fogarty, R. *The Mindful School: How to Teach for Metacognitive Reflection.* Palatine, IL: IRI/Skylight Publishing, Inc., 1994.

Gardner, H. *Frames of Mind: The Theory of Multiple Intelligences.* New York: Harper Collins, 1983.

Lazear, D. *Seven Ways of Teaching: The Artistry of Teaching with Multiple Intelligences.* Palatine, IL: IRI/Skylight Publishing, Inc., 1992.

———. *Seven Way of Knowing: Teaching for Multiple Intelligences.* Palatine, IL: IRI/Skylight Publishing, 1992.

Naisbitt, J. *Megatrends.* New York: Warner Books, Inc., 1991.

Prentice, M. *Catch Them Learning: A Handbook of Classroom Strategies.* Palatine, IL: IRI/Skylight Publishing, Inc., 1994.

Restak, R. *The Brain Has a Mind of Its Own: Insights from a Practicing Neurologist.* New York: Crown Trade Paperbacks, 1991.

———. *Receptors.* New York: Bantam Books, 1994.

Sternberg, R.J. *Beyond IQ: A Triarchic Theory of Human Intelligence.* New York: Cambridge University Press, 1985.

MIA–ADC

 M OTIVATE

 I NTEGRATE

 A SSOCIATE

 A CTIVATE

 D EMONSTRATE

 C OMMUNICATE

MIA-ADC

Motivate

To motivate students, we need to approach subject matter from the preadolescent's perception and real-world experiences. Members of this turbulent age group invest in issues, things, and goals that they relate to personally. Although they live in the "now" time frame, we must present curriculum so that they understand the long-range implications and possible applications of newly acquired information. When students realize the value of their learning, they will commit wholeheartedly to the learning process.

When introducing a new topic, theme, or unit, we may use any number of strategies to obtain the essential student link. Focusing questions work well to initiate or generate student discussions about teacher-selected topics. The insight gained from the use of focusing questions is helpful, as we make the critical judgments required for effective teaching. It also enables preadolescents to chart their own growth from their experience knowledge base to new aspects of any selected topic.

Essentially this motivational approach is student-focused, progressing from the known to the unknown. Students during this developmental period need to realize they already know something about the topic and are not starting from ground zero. They need to feel safe, secure, and anchored in their learning. Within the Motivate component of the MIA-ADC model, starting with what students already know is nonnegotiable because it creates a sense of excitement by fanning the sparks already present within the emerging self. It also provides us with critical information, such as who already knows a great deal about the topic, or who is obviously not very interested in it. The Motivate component of MIA-ADC links real-world and future goals. With this knowledge, we can authentically involve students.

Integrate

Learning has to make sense to the learner. It is through the integration of the disciplines that learning takes advantage of how the brain accommodates new information.

There are various approaches or methods for integration. For example:

1. You may want to explore a theme in one subject and make reference back to the theme throughout various lessons in different content areas. This method assists students in connecting a single theme or concept to different subjects as it promotes an understanding of the theme.

2. You may be able to integrate a theme holistically in various subject areas. In this approach, an abstract concept such as "power" can be

integrated into subjects taught by other team members.

You also must cultivate the wide range of intelligences present in every class through one of the various approaches found in the current literature. For purposes of the MIA-ADC model, Howard Gardner's multiple intelligences have been selected: verbal/linguistic, visual/spatial, auditory/musical,

bodily/kinesthetic, mathematical/logical, interpersonal, and intrapersonal.

The integration of subjects and modes of learning allows preadolescents to transfer concepts from one discipline to another, as well as to apply their learning from one problem setting to another within both academic and real-world situations. Integration is critical for the preadolescent because, through this curriculum approach, the various interest and brain-patterning tendencies are focused to accommodate their individual differences.

Associate

Associate refers to the different types of instructional settings through which a preadolescent may learn: whole-group, small-group, cooperative-group, team, or individual assignment. We need to recognize and validate the critical importance of the peer structure in the classroom when forming grouping assignments. The appropriate use of peer support can become a powerful tool for learning within this age group.

Preadolescents need to know how to function effectively in every type of grouping pattern. Changing times and roles will require them, as adults, to understand appropriate behaviors and essential skills in order to accomplish specific tasks or goals. Therefore, each student should participate in various types of grouping patterns at some time during the school year.

We who teach at the middle school and junior high level need to make sure the selected grouping patterns facilitate the objectives of instruction and are compatible with the activity to be addressed. This should be a conscious decision based on our assessment of the learner and the goals of that specific instruction. The vital issue is the match

of the goal or purpose with the selected grouping pattern. The question becomes, does it enhance learning for this specific assigned task?

Activate

Significant studies have determined that the more actively involved the preadolescent is with the learning, the greater the actual retention of the learning. It is our responsibility to chart the most appropriate learning course for students. Gardner's theory of intelligences provides a practical guide for active involvement in this process.

The first step of activate involves choosing a concept. The concept is a significant *abstract*, such as "change," "power," or "courage," which is obviously applicable to several disciplines.

With the second step, we focus the concept into a theme and decide the subject areas in which to teach the selected theme.

The third step is for us to ask focusing questions, such as, what does the student need to know about the topic? This becomes the foundation for assessment.

In the fourth step, we generate a list of different activities to help students learn the concept. We need to incorporate variety of grouping patterns—whole-class, small-group, pairs, or individual activities.

The fifth step is to consider the students' learning styles: visual, auditory, or kinesthetic. Each style should be included at some point.

The sixth step is an objective review, to make sure there is a balance in style and intelligences in the number of activities.

The seventh step is to give students choices within the framework of the activities. Choices establish the active engagement of learning and create a sense of responsibility and ownership of the learning process.

With the eighth step, our role becomes that of a coach or facilitator. While the focus is on the student's choice, we is still provide the framework and expectations for appropriate behavior and completion standards of the tasks.

Demonstrate

Inevitably, preadolescents will be faced with the need to show what they've done or show how well they understand a topic. For some, this test of their knowledge may be the civil service exam or a medical entrance exam; for others, a truck driving exam. Pen-and-pencil exams are still required in certain instances. We may feel national instruments are inappropriate, but the fact remains that students need to acquire the skills of test taking. As adults entering universities or the workforce, they will have to fulfill certain requirements imposed by those various institutions.

Authentic assessment, in which students actually demonstrate their progress, offers relevance and meaning and provides the individual pacing and growth so critical during this developmental period. Emphasis is placed on complex skills and contextualized problems, with an understanding of the fact that there is not always a single correct answer.

Authentic assessment is an active construction of meaning. Sole emphasis should not be placed on students' products alone, but also on the learning process itself.

Authentic examples of learning need to be organized and presented. One way to accomplish this is through the use of portfolios, a collection of students' work that demonstrates the efforts, progress, or achievements in given areas. Thus, a whole spectrum of real-world experiences becomes evidence of the students' accomplishments.

Communicate

Students must communicate their learning to others; this promotes self-confidence and gives them ownership of the knowledge they have gained. It is through the communication process that the worth of learning becomes real,

intertwined with a sense of accomplishment and pride.

Communication, verbal or nonverbal, is the process that objectifies learning. When the student has been actively engaged with an abstract idea or problem and has focused energies to achieve a goal, learning becomes concrete—a real product of the mind. The process inevitably provides insight into themselves and others.

Communication invites students to reach out to a world rich in unknowns and ultimately to grow intellectually and emotionally. The value of *my* efforts, *my* learning, takes on a new dimension, a new meaning, as it is communicated effectively to another. At some level, the feedback provides students with a desire to know more, become more. Thus, the value of learning meets a fundamental need to become aware of *my* abilities, *my* potentials. This need is not to be confused with self-centeredness, as such awareness will be required for a successful life. Awareness of one's own abilities and potential is especially critical in the midst of this time of self-doubts.

Summary

Every one of us working in a middle or junior high school is acutely aware of the need to help the preadolescent focus on learning, even in the midst of the demands of this developmental period. The model in this chapter is a response to that need. Most of us working with this age group wish to pool our efforts, insights, creative ideas, and various perspectives in order to provide the best school environment possible. After all, we share three common goals:

1. To help the preadolescent become a confident learner

2. To assist each preadolescent to become aware of his or her unique abilities

3. To provide opportunities for positive relationships to develop in the process

At every age and stage of life, all of us need to be astute learners, aware of our unique abilities, and have persons who care about us.

References

Gardner, H. *Frames of Mind: The Theory of Multiple Intelligences.* New York: Harper Collins, 1983.

Prentice, M. *Catch Them Learning: A Handbook of Classroom Strategies.* Palatine, IL: IRI/Skylight Publishing, Inc., 1994.

Introduction to Units

Curriculum Development Process

These units offer a wide variety of formats and styles of curriculum development. However, they share the following fundamental principles:

1. The individuals or teams of writers used the MIA-ADC construct. In some cases, the teams wrote together. In other cases, individuals wrote specific units in the same format to share with other team members.

2. The building level or operating schedule of each school influences the use of the units. Schools using block schedules rather than class periods will find this format works well because of the multiple options from which to choose.

3. Some select states currently use frameworks, and others use standards to achieve learner outcomes. The model is designed for both. It minimizes the paperwork or documentation of standards. Districts using learner outcomes will recognize the value of designing original units specifically linked to the learner outcomes.

4. It should be noted that all units were submitted by individuals teaching at the middle school or junior high level. All have been field-tested. The authors represent a wide range of school sizes and geographical areas.

5. While all activities may be used for specific assessment of student progress, the evaluation standard must be clearly articulated and well understood by teacher and students prior to beginning the unit. Some activities will be appropriate for inclusion in portfolios, others will be compatible with the more traditional, standardized forms of assessment and/or evaluation.

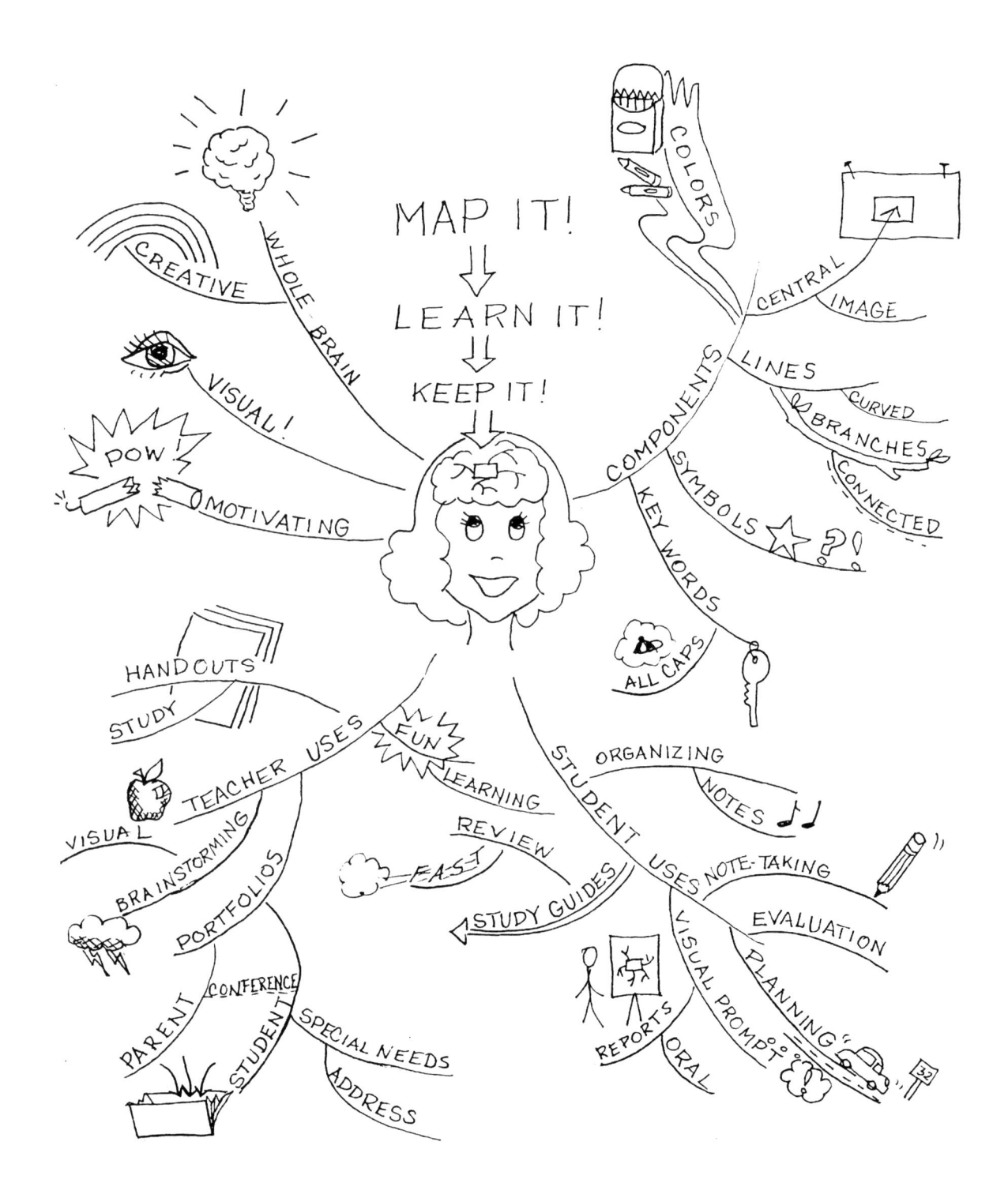

Map It! Learn It! Keep It!

Map It! Learn It! Keep It!

By Judith Bynum

Mind Mapping: A Skill to Integrate Curriculum

For many students, the traditional style of writing ideas in linear fashion on lined paper is deeply ingrained by their middle school years. With today's focus on higher-order thinking and teaching to all learning modalities, both teachers and students need an alternative method of organizing information. Mind mapping, a form of visual note taking created by Tony Buzan in 1983, allows students to use both hemispheres of the brain to better process information and aid memory retention (Clark, 1986).

A mind map allows a great deal of information to be recorded on one page while showing relationships among concepts and ideas. With thoughts focused in essential key words and with many concepts presented by single symbols, it is a concise and powerful learning tool. Since students are challenged to record ideas with symbols and color as well as words, they must use whole-brain processing (Margulies, 1991). Most graphic organizers are left-brained activities, using only words with no color.

Mind mapping is especially helpful to students who are hearing impaired, since it is a language that is both visual and conceptual. Dyslexic and learning disabled students also benefit greatly from this nonlinear approach to expressing their ideas (Margulies, 1991). Gifted and talented students respond to mind mapping's freedom of form in generating ideas visually and nonsequentially. Therefore, all students will benefit from this method of recording information that promotes, not restricts, creativity and nurtures thinking skills (Margulies, 1991).

For teachers, the best approach to mind mapping is to first learn it, then teach it. Mind mapping is not only a good method for organizing ideas and information visually, but also an excellent tool for project planning and student evaluation. Those students who have always loved to sketch and doodle while listening will embrace mind xmapping with enthusiasm, generating new excitement in the classroom.

Motivate

Ask students what they know about how the brain works. Draw a brain on the board, or use a handout, showing left and right hemispheres. Identify functions of each hemisphere and label them, using only black markers to label the left functions, and a variety of colors with symbols to label the right.

Discuss what elements of learning use each hemisphere of the brain. Can the class think of skills that use both sides simultaneously? Why would a whole-brain approach to learning be more productive and successful than an approach that only addresses one hemisphere of the brain?

Hand out a list of difficult vocabulary words chosen for their complexity, with definitions listed. Give students a short time to study the list, and then take it away and ask students to write the definitions of as many of these words as they can in five minutes. Let them know this is an experiment, not a test. Allow students to self-grade their efforts and discuss with them problems encountered in remembering the definitions.

Next, give students the same words, with simplified, key-word definitions, as well as colored symbols for the words. Allow five minutes of study time, then once again ask students to write the definitions. After grading these, allow students to share the differences in their two scores (not the scores themselves). Why did the majority of the students score higher the second time? How does this relate to what they now know about the brain?

Tell students they will be learning a whole-brain skill, which can be used in all classes, for organizing information and heightening memory. For this study, colored markers and oversized, unlined paper (10" × 13") will be needed. At the end of class, ask students to write an evaluative sentence on the vocabulary-memory experiment.

Integrate

This unit integrates language arts, math, science, and social studies. The activities make use of visual, verbal, interpersonal, and mathematical/logical intelligences.

Associate

This unit includes independent activities, such as drawing mind maps, writing short stories, and keeping a learning log. Students will get together in small groups to draw mind maps and present them to the class. The class as a whole will participate in chalkboard mind mapping, brainstorming, and discussion of activities.

Activate

Starred items * are *essential* in learning the mind mapping process. The other activities will augment the students' level of comfort and confidence in the skill. The activities are appropriate for all subject domains, with the intelligences interwoven as an integral component of each. Grouping patterns are flexible.

Symbols, Key Words, Color

Mind mapping uses symbols, key words, and colors to create a billboard effect in the brain. The following activities will lead the students to use these elements effectively.

1. Picture an image of "school." Simplify it. Draw the symbol. Brainstorm symbols

found in the school and the community. Write your feelings about the activity in your learning log.

*2. Using Activity Sheet 1 as a guide, practice drawing simple faces, symbols, and signs. Remember, the idea is to get the essence of a concept, not to draw a beautiful picture. Add your thoughts on this process to your learning log.

3. Draw a symbol for money on your paper. Add it to the blackboard for brainstorming. Change the symbol to mean "lots of money" or "a little money." Discuss drawings that have the essence of these meanings.

*4. Practice drawing the central image for the mind map. Draw a person holding a sign, a symbol for "goals," and a symbol for "summertime." Add your thoughts about this activity to your learning log.

5. Draw arrows that show feelings—a strong arrow, a quick arrow, a curved arrow, a lightning arrow.

6. Concrete nouns aren't the only words whose meanings can be captured in a drawing. Draw pictures depicting three of the following words: power, cold, hot, fat, fast, idea, deep, look, help, tall, tiny.

*7. Key words must be written in capital letters, using only one or two words to convey their meanings. Practice changing sentences to key words, and, conversely, key words back to sentences, using the mind map at the beginning of this unit. Write a paragraph in your learning log on this activity. Was it easier or harder for you to do than drawing symbols?

*8. Write a paragraph that includes specific information about yourself. Using only key words on branches drawn from your name in the center of the page, list the information in capital letters. Note in your learning log whether you feel comfortable with this type of organizational method.

9. Color a lightbulb three different ways, to signify three different concepts. Discuss.

10. Draw a picture of "creativity" using no words, only colors and symbols. Use colored markers to intensify words or symbols.

Steps to Mind Mapping

*1. To begin your first mind map, select a topic to mind map, such as plans for the day, goals for the year, or highlights of a book you've read recently. Draw a picture or symbol that represents that topic in the center of a blank, oversized piece of paper. Keep the picture small so that there is still room for ideas. If the symbol's meaning is ambiguous, write one or two words next to it to clarify the meaning.

*2. Think about ideas concerning the topic you have chosen. Write key words having to do with these ideas on curved lines radiating from the central image. Continue to branch out as more words are generated from the first branch. Use only words that convey the most information.

*3. Draw symbols in color next to the key words, ideas, and concepts.

*4. Add arrows to connect certain elements of the map.

5. Redraw the map if it is not orderly and neat.

6. If concepts are sequential, use the clock concept for organization by drawing the first branch at the one-o'clock position. Radiate around the central image in clockwise order.

7. Write your thoughts about "mind mapping to learn" in your learning log.

Example: A Story

*1. After reading "The Gift of the Magi," by O. Henry, divide the class into groups to analyze the story. Every member in each group will choose one of the following areas to mind map, so that all topics will have been mind mapped in each group:

(a) Setting: Discuss the time and place of the story.

(b) Characters: Include descriptive adjectives and character development, as well as the author's attitude toward the couple.

(c) Plot: Use the clock organization method discussed above to list the major events of the story. O. Henry is famous for surprise endings—some endings have been criticized as unfair tricks. Show in the mind map whether you perceive the ending of "The Gift of the Magi" as fair or unfair, and discuss the reasons for your answer.

(d) Theme: Discuss the significance of the poverty of the couple to the theme of the story.

(e) Allusion: What is the "gift" in the title, and what does it have to do with the magi? Show its importance to plot and theme.

(f) Irony: An ironic situation is one in which the characters' actions bring about an unexpected result. Often, an ironic situation tends to belittle characters, to make them appear foolish. Show in your mind map whether this is the case with Della and Jim.

(g) Give a biographical sketch or recommend a biography of O. Henry.

2. Using mind maps as review tools, add information as the class discusses the story.

3. Using mind mapping as an evaluation tool, draw a mind map of the story, including all of the literary devices discussed in this study.

4. Write in your learning log about how mind mapping can change your method of studying a short story.

Will it help you remember facts and concepts? Using the entries in your log, write an evaluative paragraph.

Demonstrate

Portfolio Possibilities

1. Using mind maps as notes, write an essay on "The Gift of the Magi," including setting, characters, plot, theme, literary devices, and a short biography of the author.

2. Divide students into groups and have them choose a theme for their own short story. Have them mind map an outline of the story to use in an oral presentation to the class.

3. Place all mind maps done during this study in a working portfolio, with dates.

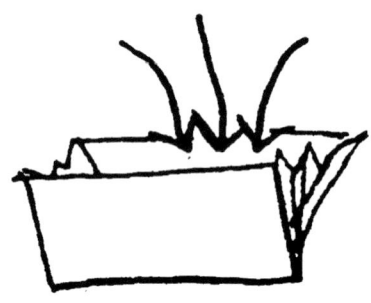

4. Have students give an oral report on another subject, using a mind map as a prompt.

5. Have students draw a wall-sized mural of what the class has learned this year in class. Divide students into groups, and choose a chapter or unit to mind map.

*6. Draw a mind map about mind mapping.

*7. Help students choose mind maps to include in a class portfolio. Ask them to write a summary of their learning processes to accompany the mind maps, using learning log notes.

Communicate

1. Display mind maps of the O. Henry story in English class.

2. Display the wall mural mind map in a school hallway for visual evaluation.

3. Ask students to use mind mapping to plan a family vacation or activity.

4. Have students teach another class or student to mind map.

5. Encourage students to show their parents the process of mind mapping through portfolio examples and the learning log summary.

Remember, English was used as an example. This strategy works well in every subject and every domain for every child.

References

Clark, B. *Optimizing Learning: The Integrative Education Model in the Classroom.* Columbus, OH: Merrill Publishing Company, 1986.

Henry, O. "The Gift of the Magi." F. Safier, ed. *Adventures in Reading.* Orlando, FL: Harcourt Brace Jovanovich, Inc., 1985

Margulies, N. *Mapping Inner Space: Learning and Teaching Mind Mapping.* Tucson, AZ: Zephyr Press, 1991.

Prentice, M. *Catch Them Learning: A Handbook of Classroom Strategies.* Palatine, IL: IRI/Skylight Publishing, Inc., 1994.

How to Mind Map

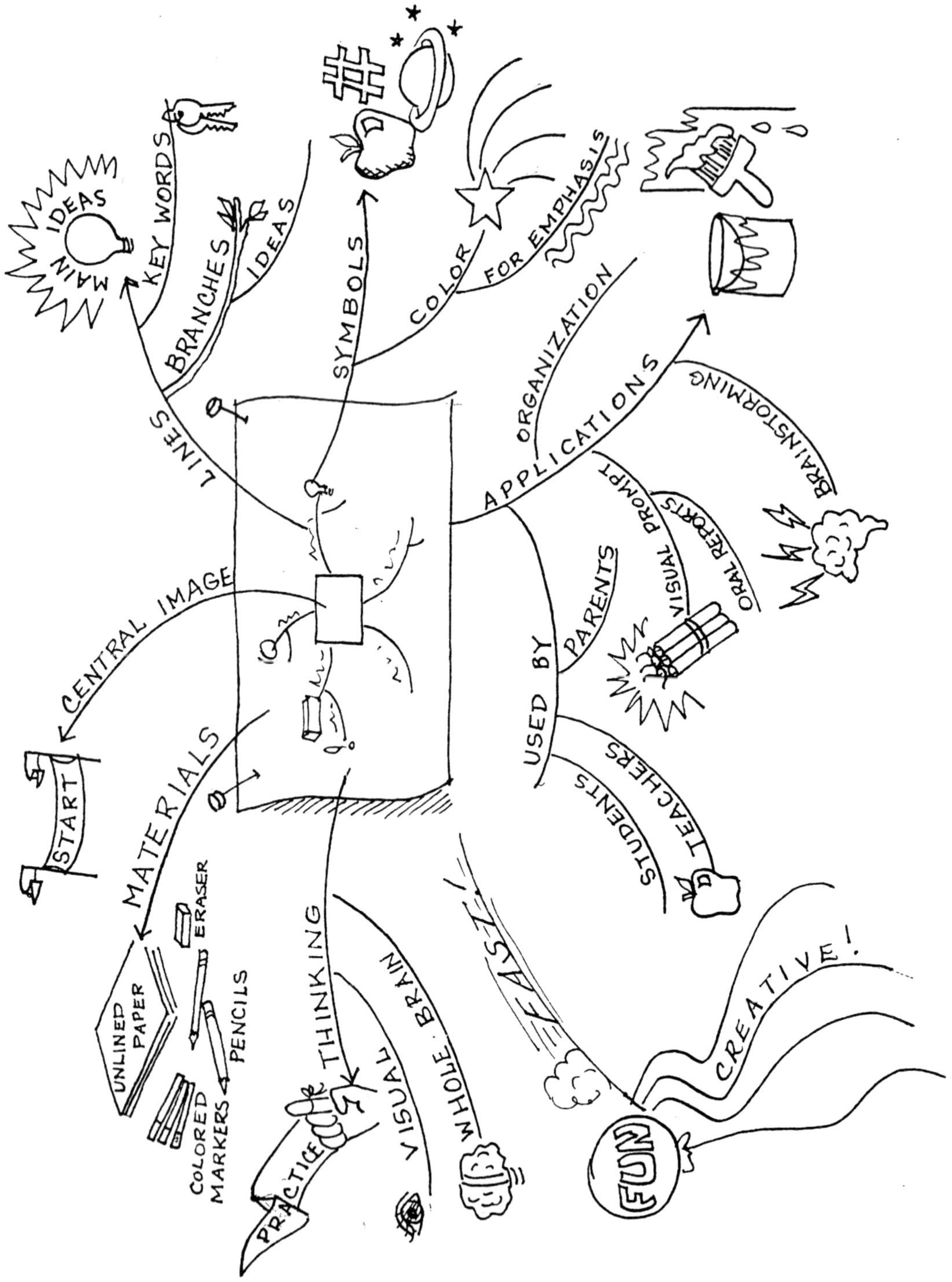

Practice Drawing Symbols

Now You Try It!

Activity Sheet

FACES:
DRAW A CIRCLE.
DRAW EYES IN CENTER, NOSE AND MOUTH BENEATH.
ADD EARS AND A CURL... A BABY!

FOR A CHILD'S FACE, DRAW HAIR; EYES HIGHER AND WIDER APART, NOSE AND MOUTH LARGER.

FOR ADULT'S FACE, DRAW OVAL;
EYES — EMPTY CIRCLES; WITH BLACK DOTS;
NOSE — A "6";
LINE FOR MOUTH;
HAIR.

A GROUP OR TEAM: DRAW SEVERAL OVALS IN A ROW.
ADD "HILLS" BELOW; PUT CURVES BEHIND HEADS TO SUGGEST LOTS OF PEOPLE.

APPLE:
DRAW AN EAR, THEN DRAW ITS MIRROR IMAGE.
ADD STEM, LEAF, AND REFLECTION.

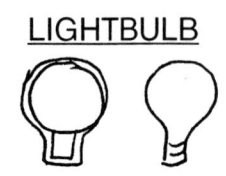

TREE

LIGHTBULB

AN AWARD:
DRAW A CIRCLE.
ADD ZIGZAG EDGE AND RIBBONS.

A BALLOON:
DRAW AN OVAL;
ADD A REFLECTION;
PUT A "W" AT THE BASE.
ADD A STRING.

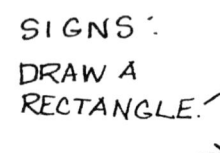

SIGNS:
DRAW A RECTANGLE.
ADD 3 FINGERS ON EACH SIDE;
ADD A HEAD AT THE TOP, WITH SHOULDERS;
WRITE MESSAGE ON SIGN.

OR

MONEY:
DRAW OVALS;
ADD BOTTOM.
SHOW MOVEMENT WITH LINES.

DOLLAR BILLS

ARROWS:

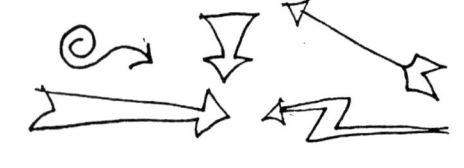

©1997 J. Weston Walch, Publisher — The Preadolescent

Eat a Dandelion

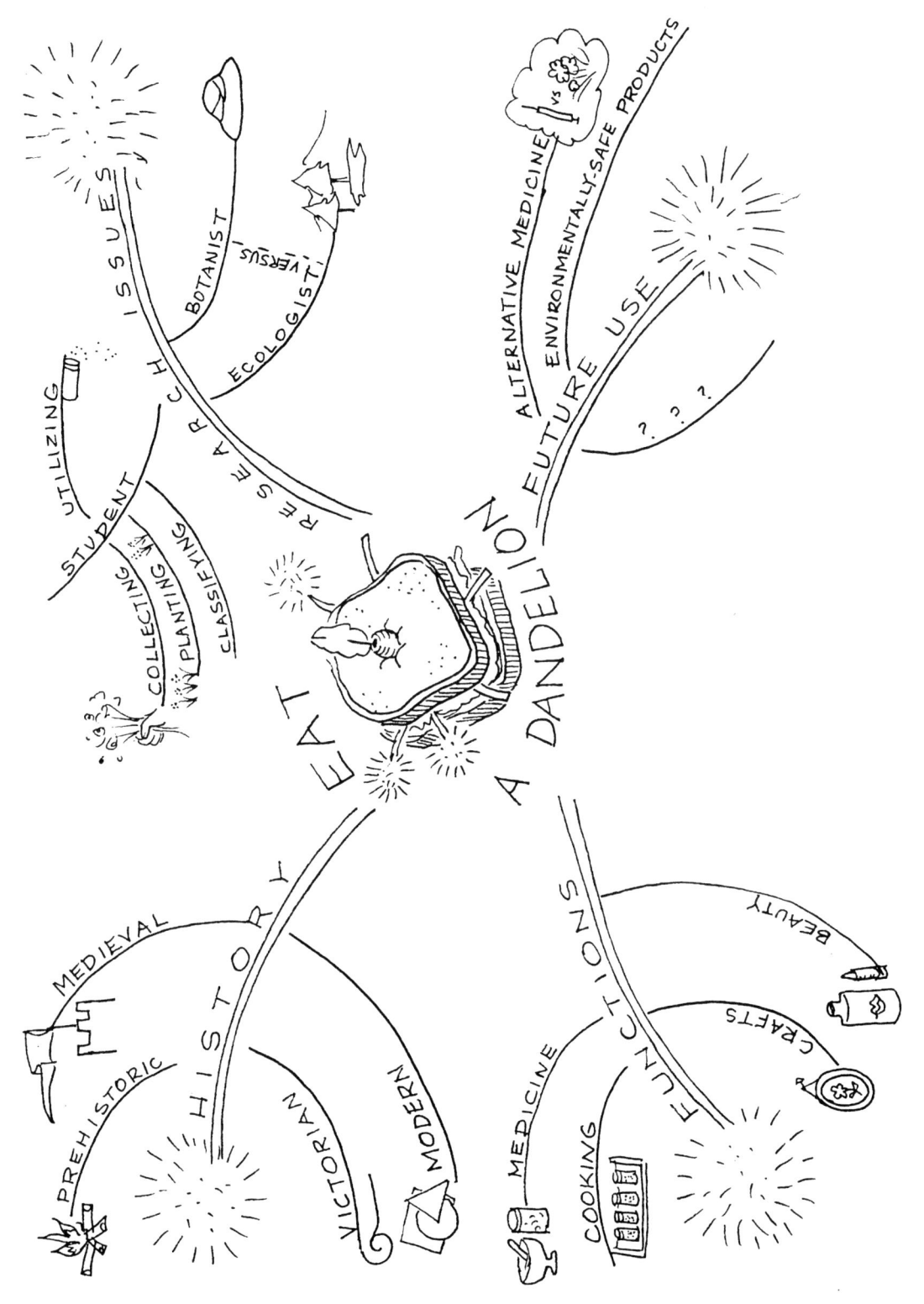

Eat a Dandelion

By Tammie Tripp-Dillion

The overall goals for this unit are:

1. To gain insight into the past and present use of herby by humans in an interdisciplinary, sensory, hands-on approach.
2. To build skills that will allow individuals to explore and appreciate their environment.

Motivate

Numerous examples of herb usage such as colorful pictures of herb gardens, medieval plant illustrations, teas, beauty products, pressed-herb pictures, and live specimens will be displayed in the room, to illustrate the many different uses for the herb. Students will play an object-awareness game in which five to seven items will be passed around the room. Students will write in their journals all of the things they think of when they look at each object. After students have written for approximately 10 minutes, the teacher will lead a discussion of what the students have written. The students will then be asked:

1. What do they believe is an herb?
2. Can simply looking at an herb tell them everything they need to know about it?
3. What might be other ways for us to learn more about herbs?
4. How many herbs can they name?

Integrate

This unit integrates social studies, science, art, and literature. Herbs are examined by studying their past and present uses, their changing definitions, and the role they may serve in the future.

Associate

Whole-group, small-group, and individual activities are found throughout the unit.

Activate

Ask students the following focusing questions:

1. What is an herb?
2. How are herbs used?
3. What skills are necessary to study herbs?
4. What might be the future role of herbs?

Many activities are offered. Teachers may select and utilize those appropriate for their individual classes.

Activities

1. **A rose is a rose.** Students will examine and dissect a wild rose and a domesticated rose. They will be asked how the two specimens differ. Other examples of wild herbs and their domestic cousins will be viewed. Students will then be asked to form a hypothesis as to why

humans have altered herbs through time. They will write their hypotheses in their journals.
Associate: whole-group
Subject: science
Intelligences: verbal/linguistic, visual/spatial

2. **Making tools.** Students will plant two types of herbs (seed-cutting, annual-perennial). Each student will have three specimens from each type at the end of the activity. These plants will be taken home, along with a project sheet that lists several experiments. Each student will perform some type of growth activity at home and display the findings and results at the authors' tea (See page 43, Communicate).
Associate: individual
Subject: science
Intelligences: visual/spatial, verbal/linguistic

3. **Growth of a seed.** Students will act out the growth of a seed into a plant, using verbal imagery provided by the instructor.
Associate: whole-group
Subject: science
Intelligences: bodily/kinesthetic

4. **Making the familiar unfamiliar.** Using a variety of activities to build awareness (looking through frames, lying on the ground for a close-up view, looking through their legs, touching without looking, etc.), the students will look for herbs, under the broad definition of nonwoody plant.
Associate: whole-group
Subject: science
Intelligences: bodily/kinesthetic, visual/spatial

5. **To pick or not to pick.** Students will discuss the pros and cons of picking flowers as opposed to simple observation as a method of learning about herbs. Information on the viewpoints of botanists and ecologists on the subject will be used as a springboard for discussion.
Associate: whole-group
Subject: science
Intelligences: verbal/linguistic

6. **Playground flowers.** Lead a discussion of how all plants were once considered herbs, and present illustrations of flower-designing principles to the class. Students will then use the flower-designing principles, drinking straws embedded in modeling clay, and tiny flowers found on campus to create their own arrangements. Once the arrangements are complete, the students will have a mini flower show, judging the flowers on design criteria.
Associate: whole-group and individual
Subject: art
Intelligences: verbal/linguistic, visual/spatial

7. **Scavenger hunt.** Students will break into small groups and

try to find as many shapes as possible found in plants on campus. All students will then combine the bounty and sort examples by any classification system they develop and agree upon. Classification of plant types will be discussed.
Associate: small-group
Subject: science
Intelligences: verbal/linguistic, visual/spatial

8. **Habitats.** Give your students a brief description of the range of habitats and conditions of a location. Break students into small groups and assign a different area to each group. Have students write in their journals the things that their assigned habitat contains and the conditions that may have caused those things to appear there. The groups will share their descriptions and their theories on the various habitats. They will also discuss what things other than plants may be affected by changes in habitat.
Associate: small-group
Subject: science
Intelligences: verbal/linguistic

9. **Traveling back in time.** Students will walk back in time, using your imagery and open-ended questions. They will first visit the prehistoric period when knowledge was passed down orally and when a number of herb names were developed. Discussion will cover the common names of plants and what kinds of problems might have existed without written information concerning herb use. A list of herb names will be given to the students, who will then break into groups and discuss thoughts on how plants were given such funny names. Whole-group discussion will help categorize methods of naming (by appearance, use, etc.). Students will then find one plant, give it a name, and explain in their journals their reasons for choosing that particular name.
Associate: whole-group and small-group
Subjects: science, social studies
Intelligences: verbal/linguistic

10. **Medieval herbs.** Students will move to the medieval period, when many herbs were described and illustrated by monks. Students will be given a choice as to the herb that they would like to record (from photographs) and will use pen and herbal ink to illustrate and write a three- to four-line description of their herb. The students will have several books in class to use as examples for their written descriptions. These herb illustrations and descriptions will be combined into a

coloring book, which will be given out at the authors' tea.

Many of the students will find that their herb has traveled a long way from its place of origin. Students will brainstorm ideas on how these herbs traveled. Students will also discuss why writing about and illustrating herbs was an essential part of medieval literature.
Associate: individual
Subjects: social studies, art, language arts
Intelligences: verbal/linguistic, visual/spatial

11. **Victorian herbs.** Students will move to the Victorian period, when herbs were invested with a function that was not essential for survival. A list of herbs and their symbolic meanings will be distributed. Students will create a *tussie mussie*, a fragrant mixture, using the list and supplied fresh herbs. In their journal they will write the coded message relayed in the small arrangement.
Associate: whole-group
Subjects: social studies, science, language arts
Intelligences: verbal/linguistic

12. **Form versus function.** Using a variety of flowerpots, ask students to look at their forms and imagine how their use dictated their designs. Ask students to list the requirements of a flowerpot. Ask them to view the object as a piece of art. Read to the students Badger's viewpoint from T.H. White's *The Once and Future King*.
Associate: whole-group
Subject: social studies
Intelligences: verbal/linguistic

13. **Everything's coming up herbs.** Using the pottery assignment as a springboard, discuss how it is a symbol of humankind's taming of the earth and how the contents and arrangement of the plant world have been changed to better suit human needs.
Associate: whole-group
Subject: social studies
Intelligences: verbal/linguistic

14. **What gardens can tell us.** Using large color photos of various types of gardens and some items associated with gardens, lead students through various periods of history, using the visuals and a fictional story of one family's changing garden through medieval, Renaissance, Asian, and colonial styles. Time periods will also be indicated by students' seating posture.
Associate: whole-group
Subject: social studies
Intelligences: visual/spatial

15. **Garden design.** After the history introduction, break students into small teams and have them brainstorm a list of the different characteristics of one of the gardening styles discussed in exercise 14. Students will report their findings to the whole group and then discuss design principles used to arrange gardens.
Associate: small-group and whole group

Subjects: social studies, art
Intelligences: verbal/linguistic

16. **The centerpiece.** Students will learn the history of *topiary*, ornamental gardening, and will create a design based on past or present preferences (geometric, whimsical). These plantings will be used as center-pieces for the authors' tea.
Associate: whole-group
Subjects: social studies, art
Intelligences: visual/spatial

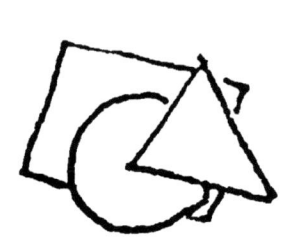

17. **Sprouting artists.** With bean sprouts planted the first day of class and black paper, students will arrange an interesting design, as a warm-up activity. Peers will comment on the arrangement.
Associate: individual
Subject: art
Intelligences: visual/spatial

18. **Theme gardening.** Using photos from exercise 14, discuss different types of gardens based on themes (bee, hummingbird, Shakespeare, color, etc.). Students will then create their own three-dimensional garden model, using a variety of materials. Plenty of room for choice in design and material should be made available.
Associate: individual
Subject: art
Intelligences: visual/spatial

19. **Dr. Herb.** Descriptions of past herbal remedies will be read from sources such as Vance Randolph (folk medicine) and old medical books. Students will learn the changing views on medical practices and beliefs. They will create a poultice based on information from an old medical book and apply it to a classmate's arm. Conduct a class discussion on how many of the past remedies have been found valid, and what that might mean for the future, given the current lack of whole plant communities. Warn students of the danger of some herbs. Make sure they understand that the medicinal use of herbs should be approached carefully.
Associate: whole-group and individual
Subjects: social studies, science
Intelligences: visual/spatial

20. **Beauty and the herb.** Students will become consumer researchers and will experiment with a number of beauty products found on today's market ("actibath" in tiny pools, facial masks, etc.). Students will then travel to the past and, using sixteenth-century recipes, create their own soap. Give students information on past hygiene practices, and discuss why people of the past made their own products. Students can try some of the past methods of hygiene during this discussion, such as brushing their teeth with sage. Students will learn when beauty products began to

be marketed.
Associate: whole-group
Subjects: social studies, science
Intelligences: visual/spatial, verbal/linguistic

21. **Scratch, sniff, and eat.** Using 12 different culinary herbs, students will sniff or taste a leaf from each kind and write in their journal three thoughts that come to mind. Invite students to read their thoughts to the class, then ask students to look under their chairs, where you have placed the herb they will be responsible for researching and presenting at the authors' tea.
Associate: whole-group
Subject: language arts
Intelligences: verbal/linguistic

22. **Chef Herb.** Students will learn about the different parts of herbs that are edible by tasting seeds, leaves, stems, and flowers—either alone or with food. Students will learn which herbs are used in the culinary arts by creating their own personal recipe for a bouquet garnish, using dried and fresh herbs. Ask students to compare the differences in appearance, smell, etc., between the fresh and dried herbs. Students will discuss why they believe herbs are used as seasonings and how they might affect our health. Some herbs are also used as sweeteners. Allow students to choose a flavor of mint to taste and describe to the class. Students will then select one of the mints to flavor their homemade jelly.
Associate: whole-group
Subject: science
Intelligences: verbal/linguistic

23. **Around the world in eight dishes.** Students will explore regional herb blends by tasting various foods from eight countries and trying to detect the herbs used in cooking each food. (Each dish will have three herbs listed. Books for research will be made available.) Students will then use fruits, vegetables, and herbs to create their own ethnic dish. Have students write their secret recipe in their journals. Students will then sample the dishes and decide on two or three to serve at the authors' tea. Discuss with students theories on why there are regional differences in the types of herbs used for cooking.
Associate: whole-group and individual
Subjects: science, social studies
Intelligences: verbal/linguistic, visual/spatial

24. **Aroma to kill vampires.** Discuss with students the past and present uses of potpourri. Give them five different blends of potpourri to smell, and ask

them to write their thoughts about each in their journals. Students will then make their own personal charm to ward off vampires or disease, in imitation of two popular historical uses of potpourri.
Associate: whole-group
Subjects: social studies, science
Intelligences: visual/spatial

25. **Potpourri production line.** Discuss with students the different methods employed in a small craft versus a factory production. Split the class in half, with one group functioning as a factory and the other group creating a craft. Give the groups 15 minutes to create potpourri balls. The groups will then discuss the different methods of construction used and the quality of each product. Lead students in a discussion of when each method of production is appropriate, based on what they have just learned. The class will then form a small business, creating and marketing a class potpourri, which they will develop. The potpourri will be put out for the authors' tea.
Associate: small-group
Subject: social studies
Intelligences: verbal/linguistic, visual/spatial

26. **Crafty herbs.** Students will discuss the different forms of art (fine, commercial, and craft), with emphasis on the reasons why each exists. (Examples using herbs will be introduced to illustrate concepts.) Students will then learn about the important role that baskets played in the past. Students will create a basket, choosing from two types of design (one circular basket made with vines and long-stemmed herbs, and one square basket made with cattails).
Associate: whole-group
Subjects: social studies, art
Intelligences: verbal/linguistic, visual/spatial

27. **Papermaking and pressed flowers.** Students will learn of the past use of plants in papermaking. They will also learn about protecting various resources by recycling and reuse. They will create their own scented paper and decorate it with flowers they have collected and pressed in their herbarium.
Associate: whole-group
Subjects: social studies, art
Intelligences: visual/spatial

28. **Should I mow or let it grow?** Have students take on various professional roles, such as medical researcher, naturalist, botanist, etc., and debate the fate of a field that contains wild herbs. Teach students about a state program that tries to reseed and recapture the floral diversity once existed in your area. Then give students the opportunity to replant wild herbs along the roadside. Preservation, rehabilitation, and what is lost forever are the themes of this lesson.
Associate: individual
Subjects: science, social studies
Intelligences: bodily/kinesthetic, verbal/linguistic, visual/spatial

Demonstrate

Portfolio Possibilities

Have students create a three- to five-minute oral presentation on the results of their growth experiment. They should also submit their presentation in any approved written format. Class presentations will use verbal and visual skills.

In addition, ask students to develop a mini info-commercial on some aspect of the use of their assigned herbs.

Communicate

Students will present their work at an authors' tea. The class coloring books will be distributed and authors will sign them. Photos and autobiographies will be on display. Students will give their findings on the growth experiments and a brief report on their assigned herb. Parents will be invited to share in the celebration.

References

Ausubel, K. *Seed of Change.* San Francisco: Harper, 1994.

Bayard, T. *Sweet Herbs and Sundry Flowers.* New York: Metropolitan Museum of Art, 1983.

Beston, H. *Herbs and the Earth.* David Godine, 1935.

Bilsky, L. *Historical Ecology.* Kennikat Press, 1980.

Bremness, L. *The Complete Book of Herbs.* Viking Studio Books, 1988.

Brown and Douglas. *A Garden Heritage.* Arkansas Territorial Restoration Foundation, 1983.

Cronon, W. *Changes in the Land.* Hill and Wang, 1983.

Crosby, A. *Ecological Imperialism.* Cambridge University Press, 1986.

Cunningham, S. *Encyclopedia of Magical Herbs.* Llewellyn Publications, 1973.

Douglas, Frey, et al. *Garden Design.* Simon and Schuster, 1974.

Garland, S. *The Herb Garden.* Penguin Books, 1984.

Gallup and Reich. *The Complete Book of Topiary.* Workman Publishing, 1987.

Herman, Passineau, et al. *Teaching Kids to Love the Earth.* Pfeifer-Hamilton, 1991.

Hunken, J. *Botany for All Ages.* Globe Pequot Press, 1989.

Hutchens, A. *A Handbook of Native American Herbs.* Shambhala, 1992.

Johnson, A. *Sketching in Nature.* Sierra Club Books, 1990.

Kenda and Williams. *Cooking Wizardry for Kids.* Barrons, 1990.

Kent and Steward. *Learning by Heart.* Bantam Books, 1992.

Klein and Klein. *Discovering Plants.* Natural History Press, 1968.

Kohl and Gainer. *Good Earth Art*. Bright Ring Publishing, 1991.

Loewer, P. *American Gardens*. Simon and Schuster, 1991.

Marranca, B. *American Garden Writing*. Penguin Books, 1988.

Massey, E. *Bittersweet Earth*. University of Oklahoma Press, 1985.

Miller, L. *Arkansas Wildflowers*. White Publishing, 1977.

Oster, M. *Gifts and Crafts from the Garden*. Rodale Press, 1988.

Pollan, M. *Second Nature*. Dell Publishing, 1991.

Prentice, M. *Catch Them Learning: A Handbook of Classroom Strategies*. Palatine, IL: IRI/Skylight Publishing, Inc., 1994

Prittied, J. *The Crafter's Garden*. Meredith Press, 1993.

Renzulli, J. *Systems and Models for Developing Programs for the Gifted and Talented*. Creative Learning Press, 1986.

Rodales. *Illustrated Encyclopedia of Herbs*. Rodale Press, 1987.

Shaudys, P. *Herbal Treasures*. A Garden Way Book, 1990.

———. *The Pleasure of Herbs*. A Garden Way Book, 1986.

Taylor, C. *Herbal Wreaths*. Sterling Lark Books, 1992.

Voris, Sedzielarz, and Blackmon. *Teach the Mind: Touch the Spirit*. Field Museum of Natural History, 1986.

Weiss, G. *The Healing Herbs*. Wings Books, 1985.

Herbal Time Travel

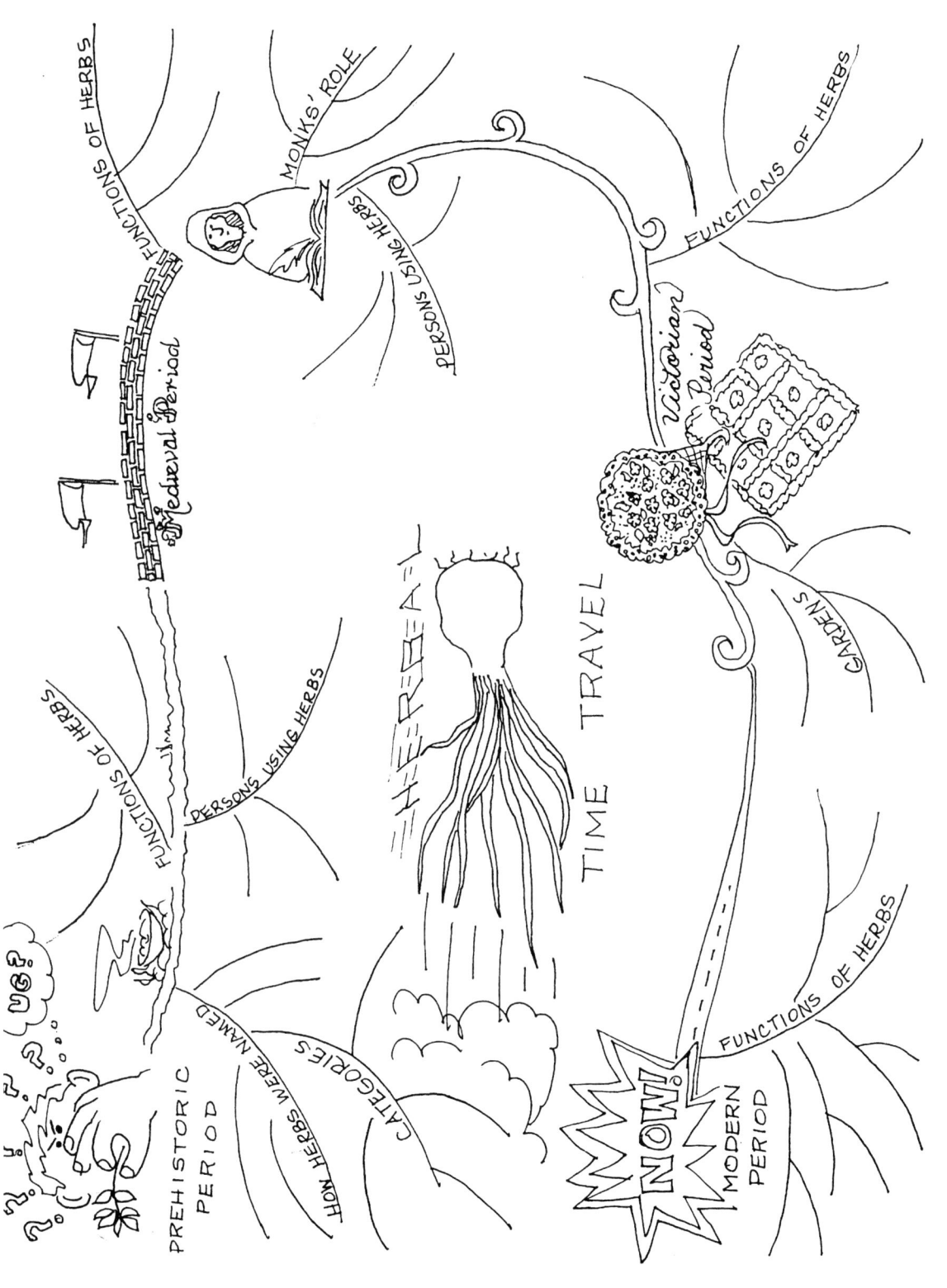

Herbs

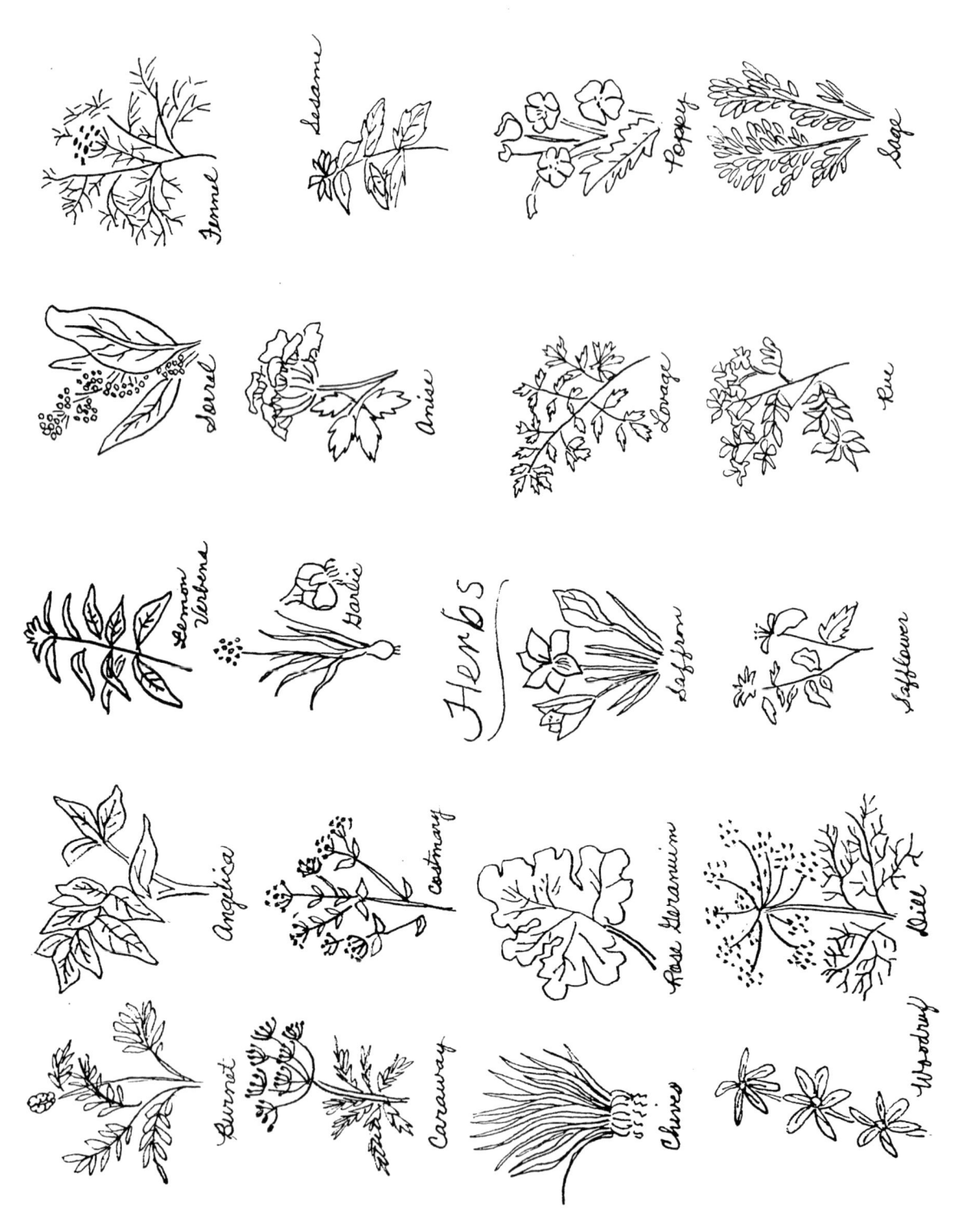

Should I Mow . . . or Let It Grow?

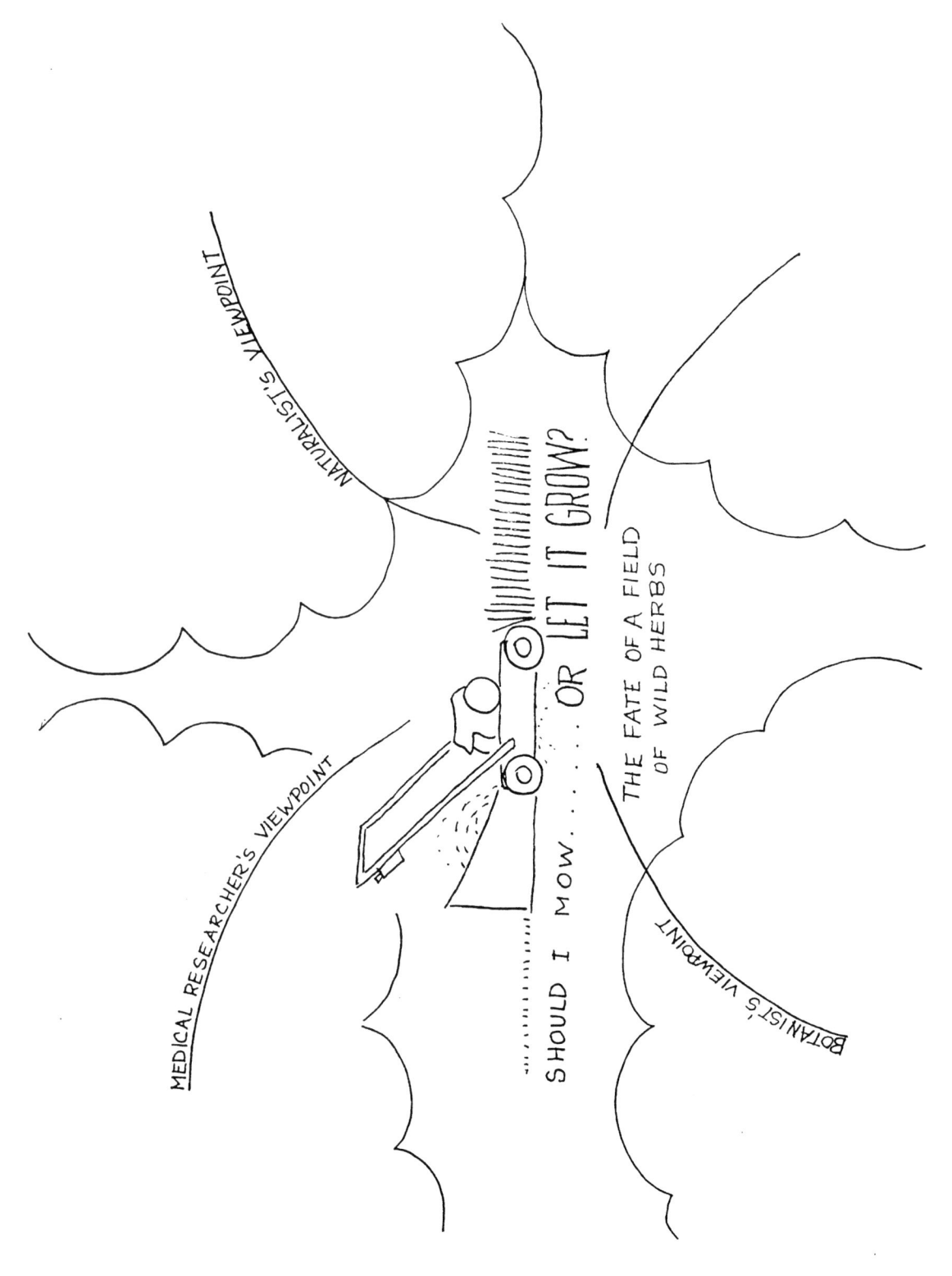

NATURALIST'S VIEWPOINT

MEDICAL RESEARCHER'S VIEWPOINT

OR LET IT GROW?

THE FATE OF A FIELD OF WILD HERBS

SHOULD I MOW . . .

BOTANIST'S VIEWPOINT

Architecture: The Structure of Our Lives

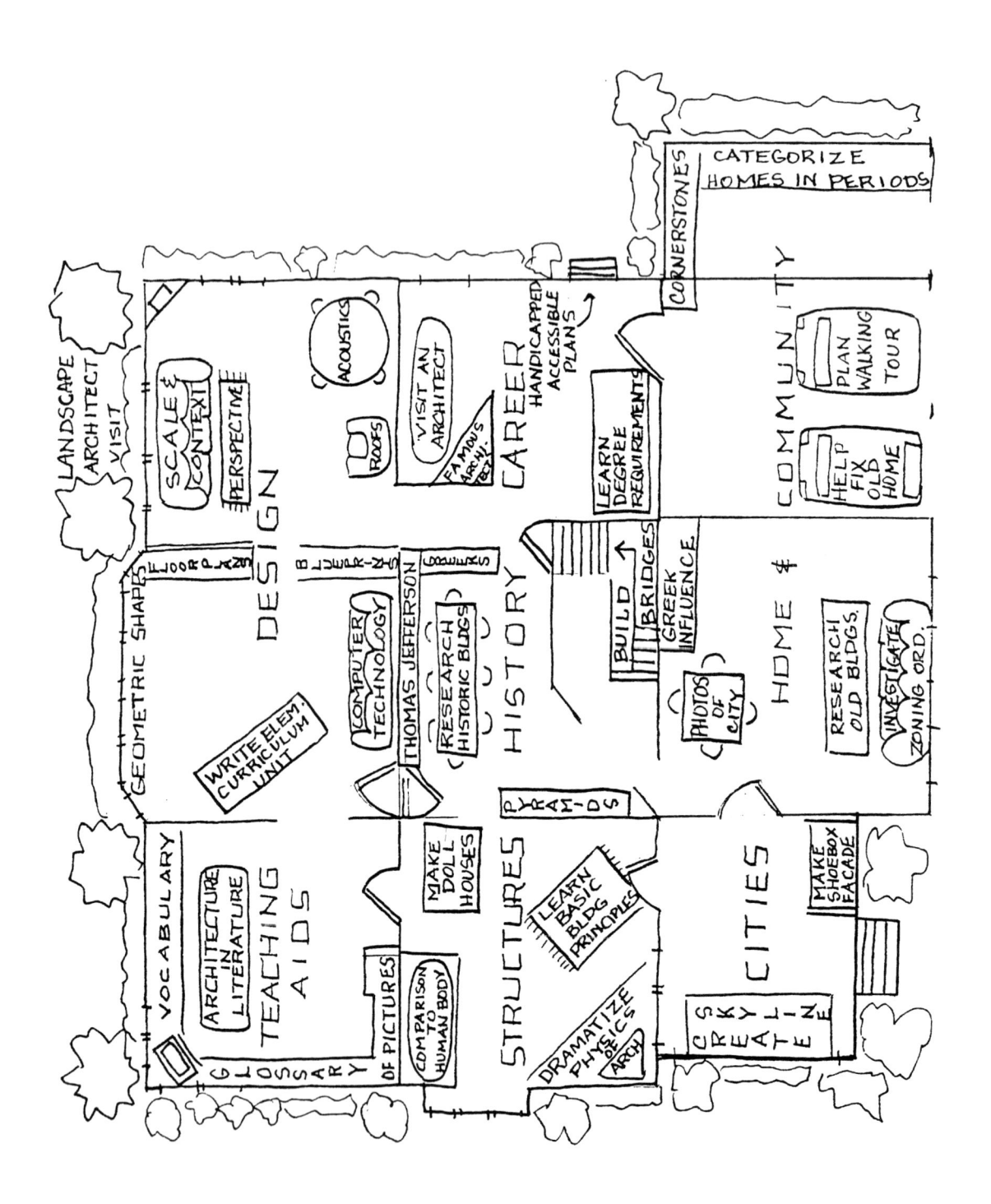

Architecture: The Structure of Our Lives

By Judith Bynum

Our present culture is very concerned with the environment. We want to preserve rare species of flora and fauna, to have unpolluted air and water, and to enjoy pristine forests and wilderness areas. Many of the priceless parts of our architectural environmental heritage, the buildings of our past, have also become rare species in need of protection. Natural predators in the form of business, government, building codes, demolition crews, remodelers, and modernizers continue to destroy this cultural heritage in the name of progress (Winters, 1986).

Two issues in protecting our buildings have come to the forefront: one is the preservation of our rich cultural genealogy; the other is preservation of the future environment. The best hope in both areas lies in helping students to become visually literate (Winters, 1986). Teaching students to understand the factors involved in shaping our environment will help them participate in its development, as well as motivate them to become involved in changing it. This is essential to the survival of our culture (Abhau, 1986).

The study of architecture involves many disciplines: history, science, math, engineering, art, social studies, psychology, philosophy, computer science, and law. This type of study teaches students to become visual thinkers. Since it is experimental, architecture is rewarding to teach. Almost any approach to architecture may be followed, as there are so many environments from which to choose: home, school, community, downtown, historic environments of the past, or well-known architectural monuments of the world. Through creating scale drawings, using photography, writing stories, interviewing people, taking field trips, building models, measuring, counting, and observing, architecture becomes important to students (Abhau, 1986).

Options in this unit are varied. The Activate element offers opportunities to select those activities that are appropriate for classroom objectives, structures, and time factors.

Motivate

Read aloud to the class *Bridges Go from Here to There,* by Forrest Wilson. This book addresses basic engineering principles involved in bridge construction. After listening to the story, the class will discuss how bridges are strengthened and lengthened. Then they will be assigned to pair-share groups to plan and construct a tongue-depressor bridge that will carry the greatest weight. Only tongue depressors and metal brads will be used for materials. (Ideally, the class will have a weekend to work and then a class competition will be staged.)

Integrate

This unit integrates math, language arts, social studies, and science. Logical/mathematical, verbal/linguistic, visual/spacial, and interpersonal intelligences will be utilized throughout the unit.

Associate

This unit includes independent study activities such as reading, researching, and performing experiments. Students will get into pairs during the bridge-building and drawing activities. Small groups will be formed for the purposes of conducting projects, the scavenger hunt, and the dramatization of architectural terms. The class as a whole will watch videos and participate in discussions, field trips, and vocabulary studies.

Activate

1. Read the first chapter of *The House of the Seven Gables*, by Nathaniel Hawthorne. Using clues found in the text, draw a picture of the house as accurately as possible. Discuss the significance of the house's architectural features to the plot of the story. What other novel have you read that uses architecture as part of the plot?
   Associate: independent
   Subject: language arts
   Intelligences: verbal/linguistic, visual/spatial, logical/mathematical

2. Read *Three Little Pigs*. Creatively change the architecture of the pigs' houses to include specific architectural elements. Using information you have learned about gravity, mass, weight, compression, and tension, describe the outcome of the Big Bad Wolf's huffing and puffing on the newly designed pig homes.
   Associate: independent or small-group
   Subject: language arts
   Intelligences: verbal/linguistic

3. Fill a box with slips of paper bearing individual architectural terms. Choose a slip from the box. For the next day's assignment, define the term for the class, using creative ways to help them remember it.
   Associate: whole-class
   Subject: language arts
   Intelligences: verbal/linguistic, visual/spatial, bodily/kinesthetic

4. Refer to the dictionary and encyclopedia as you find unfamiliar terms during your study. Keep an architectural illustrated glossary by drawing pictures of new terms and recording their definitions.
   Associate: independent or whole-class
   Subject: language arts
   Intelligences: verbal/linguistic, visual/spatial

5. Take photographs of local architecture during a neighborhood walk. When the prints are developed, mount them on a sheet of paper. Divide the class into teams and list all of the vocabulary words that can be found in the pictures.
   Associate: small-group
   Subject: language arts
   Intelligences: verbal/linguistic, visual/spatial

6. Make a large drawing of the facade of a building with examples of architectural elements. Label the architectural features.

Associate: whole-group
Subject: language arts
Intelligences: visual/spatial

7. In pairs, sit back-to-back with drawing pads and pencils. Draw pictures of structures so that your partner cannot see your work. Dictate your picture to your partner, who must re-create your original by understanding the vocabulary words. Switch roles. Compare and display.
   Associate: pair-share
   Subject: language arts
   Intelligences: visual/spatial, interpersonal

8. Show how three-dimensional shapes can be made from two-dimensional shapes (example: square and cube). Find examples of both two- and three-dimensional shapes in pictures of structures.
   Associate: whole-group
   Subject: math
   Intelligences: visual/spatial

9. Using pipe cleaners, make a human figure. Measure your figure and estimate how tall a house would have to be to fit the figure's scale. Make a drawing of the house, adjusting it to be sure that the figure fits. This teaches the concept of context.
   Associate: whole-group
   Subject: math
   Intelligences: visual/spatial

10. To understand the concept of perspective, hold a rectangle of clear plastic to act as a window. Have a partner look through the plastic and trace the lines of the image visible on the other side with a grease pencil.
    Associate: pair-share
    Subject: art
    Intelligences: visual/spatial

11. Visit a local architectural firm to see how computers are used in design.
    Associate: whole-group or individual
    Subject: computer science
    Intelligences: visual/spatial, bodily/kinesthetic

12. Under the guidance of a local architect, follow the construction of a building, from the architect's drawings to completion.
    Associate: whole-group or individual
    Subject: math
    Intelligences: logical/mathematical

13. Research and list prerequisites and courses for a degree in architecture.
    Associate: independent
    Subject: language arts
    Intelligences: verbal/linguistic

14. Research the history and architecture of a house in your community and present your findings orally and in writing.
    Associate: small-group or individual
    Subjects: language arts, social studies
    Intelligences: verbal/linguistic, visual/spatial

15. Research Thomas Jefferson's architectural accomplishments. Report your findings to the class.
    Associate: independent

Subjects: language arts, social studies
Intelligences: verbal/linguistic

16. Choose a twentieth-century architect to research for an oral presentation (example: Frank Lloyd Wright or Fay Jones).
    Associate: independent
    Subject: language arts
    Intelligences: verbal/linguistic

17. Write a curriculum unit on architecture for elementary classes or a Scout troop or club. Include major topics.
    Associate: independent
    Subjects: language arts, social studies
    Intelligences: verbal/linguistic

18. Using grid paper, rulers, and pencils, draw the front of your house. Estimate the size of the windows and doors, and the dimensions of the house. Take your drawing home, check your measurements, and correct any mistakes. In the next class, discuss the problems you had in doing this exercise and the skills you need to know to draw better technical drawings, as well as information you want to learn about architecture.
    Associate: whole-class
    Subject: math
    Intelligences: logical/mathematical, visual/spatial

19. Compare the aspects of a building to human anatomy (example: foundation = feet).
    Associate: whole-group
    Subject: science
    Intelligences: visual/spatial

20. Dramatize or mime the basic building principles of compression, tension, gravity, force, column, arch, post and lintel, dome, and flying buttress.
    Associate: small-group
    Subject: science
    Intelligences: bodily/kinesthetic

21. Using toilet paper tubes, demonstrate that a column is weak when it is lying on its side but strong when standing up. Guess how many books four tubes of equal size can support. Then carefully pile books on the tube. Was your guess accurate? Weigh the books and compare their weight to the weight of the tubes that supported them.
    Associate: small-group
    Subject: science
    Intelligences: bodily/kinesthetic, visual/spatial

22. Find examples of Doric, Ionic, and Corinthian columns in local landmarks.
    Associate: independent
    Subject: social studies
    Intelligences: visual/spatial

23. Using marshmallows and toothpicks, make the most stable structure that you can. Next, make structures that are the highest, the largest in all directions, the smallest. Compare your structures with the designs of the other students in your class.
    Associate: whole-group
    Subject: science
    Intelligences: bodily/kinesthetic

24. Investigate the energy systems in your home—the electrical, the plumbing, and the heating systems. Report your findings to the class and compare the systems in your home with the systems in the homes of your classmates.

Associate: individual and whole-group
Subject: science
Intelligences: bodily/kinesthetic

25. Acoustics, or sound control, is important in architectural design. Investigate the etymologies of the following words related to acoustics*:* amphitheater, audible, audience, audio, auditorium. What special structures and materials are used in auditoriums?
Associate: whole-group
Subjects: language arts, science
Intelligences: verbal/linguistic

26. Learn how to read a floor plan. Research the codes and symbols that architects use when making floor plans. Bring a sample floor plan to class and explain it to your classmates.
Associate: whole-group
Subject: language arts
Intelligences: visual/spatial

27. Make a shoebox facade with windows, doors, chimneys, awnings, shutters, roof, steps, etc. Make a neighborhood display by grouping everyone's facades together on a table.
Associate: small-group and whole-group
Subject: social studies
Intelligences: visual/spatial, bodily/kinesthetic

28. Check your local newspapers for real estate ads. Decipher the abbreviations in the ads and develop a list of key real estate terms. Write your own real estate ad for a home of another culture or time.
Associate: whole-group
Subject: language arts
Intelligences: verbal/linguistic

29. Investigate the zoning ordinances of your community or city and explain them to your class, using a visual/spatial display.
Associate: independent
Subject: social studies
Intelligences: verbal/linguistic, visual/spatial

30. Find interesting cornerstones or plaques on public buildings, bridges, or statues. Research their significance, and present your findings to the class.
Associate: independent
Subject: social studies
Intelligences: verbal/linguistic, bodily/kinesthetic

31. Invite a landscape architect to class to talk about his or her job.
Associate: whole-class
Subject: science
Intelligences: verbal/linguistic

32. As a class, watch the video *Castle,* by David Macaulay. Discuss the art of construction and how it has changed since the period depicted in the video.
Associate: whole-group
Subject: language arts
Intelligences: visual/spatial, verbal/linguistic

33. As a class, watch the video *Pyramid,* by David Macaulay. Compare the art of construction of today with that of the time of the pyramids.
Associate: whole-group
Subject: language arts
Intelligences: visual/spatial, verbal/linguistic

34. Think about possible reasons why pyramids were built in Egypt and in South America at the same time. Write an essay on your hypothesis.
    Associate: independent
    Subject: language arts
    Intelligences: verbal/linguistic

35. Using architectural rubber stamps, create skylines of buildings. Try to re-create a historic building.
    Associate: independent
    Subject: social studies
    Intelligences: bodily/kinesthetic, visual/spatial

36. Design an alteration to a building that is now inaccessible to the handicapped.
    Associate: independent
    Subject: social studies
    Intelligences: visual/spatial, interpersonal

37. Study roof systems so that you will be able to identify different kinds of roofs. Bring several types of hats to class. Use the hats as roofs of buildings (a baseball cap, for example, might become the roof of an astrodome).
    Associate: whole-group
    Subject: language arts
    Intelligences: visual/spatial

38. Research one significant structure from each of the general periods of architecture. Write a one-page report on each structure and draw or copy a picture to go with each report. Put the reports together to create a book of historic architecture. The general periods of architecture are: Ancient World, Early Christian, Medieval, Renaissance, Baroque, Revolutionary, and Twentieth Century.
    Associate: independent
    Subject: language arts
    Intelligences: visual/spatial, verbal/linguistic

39. Categorize 10 homes and buildings in your own community, referring to basic periods and styles of history. Use the new terms you have learned in this unit to describe the architectural details of the structures.
    Associate: whole-group
    Subject: social studies
    Intelligences: logical/mathematical

Demonstrate

Portfolio Possibilities

1. Create a booklet of the architecture of the homes in your community.

2. Plan a walking tour of your community for elementary students.

3. Design and draw plans for dollhouses. Shop classes will construct the houses. Once the houses have been built, the class will work in groups to paint and paper them.

4. Plan and execute a mission project for the class to do in your community, such as building a front porch for an elderly person.

5. Compare the architecture of ancient civilizations to present-day architecture, in style, design, and appearance. Show how architecture mirrors trends in society, how it compares with

fads in styles and fashions of different eras.

6. Write a three-page research paper on a significant historical architectural wonder.

7. Draw blueprints of your dream house. Construct it to scale, using plywood or fiberboard for walls. Plan the interior and exterior designs, using both texture and color. Landscape a yard around your model house.

Communicate

1. Take elementary students on a walking tour of the community to learn about the architecture of your area. Prepare students for the trip and act as their guide.

2. Present the dollhouses you have designed to a local children's home or homeless shelter.

3. Video-tape your class mission project in progress, and show it to other classes or to local service organizations.

4. Share your research papers on architecturally significant structures with other classes.

5. Make a neighborhood of class dream houses in a large room. Add streets, landscaping, stop signs, parks, and other interesting features. Hold an open house, and invite your parents to visit your homemade town.

References

Abhau, M. *Architecture in Education: A Resource of Imaginative Ideas and Tested Activities.* Philadelphia: Foundation for Architecture, 1986.

Foundation for Architecture. Courtenay-Thompson, F., ed. New York: Dorling Kindersley, Inc., 1986.

Eisen, D. *Fun with Architecture.* New York: The Metropolitan Museum of Art, 1992.

Hawthorne, N. *The House of the Seven Gables.* Oxford: Oxford University Press, 1951.

Lewis, A. *Super Structures.* New York: The Viking Press, 1979.

Macaulay, D. *Castle.* (video) Boston: Houghton Mifflin, 1977.

Macaulay, D. *Pyramid.* (video) Boston: Houghton Mifflin, 1975.

Petranek, S., and J. Allen. "A House for All America." *Life.* June 1994, pp. 82–98.

Prentice, M. *Catch Them Learning: A Handbook of Classroom Strategies.* Palatine, IL.: IRI/Skylight Publishing, Inc., 1994.

Whitney, C. B*ridges: Their Art, Science, and Evolution.* New York: Greenwich House, 1983.

Wilson, F. *Bridges Go from Here to There.* Washington, D.C.: The Preservation Press, 1993.

Winters, N. *Architecture Is Elementary: Visual Thinking Through Architectural Concepts.* Salt Lake City, UT: Gibbs-Smith, Publisher, 1986.

Young Architects. (kit) Patail Enterprises, Inc.

Zemach, M. *Three Little Pigs.* Canada: Harper Collins, 1996.

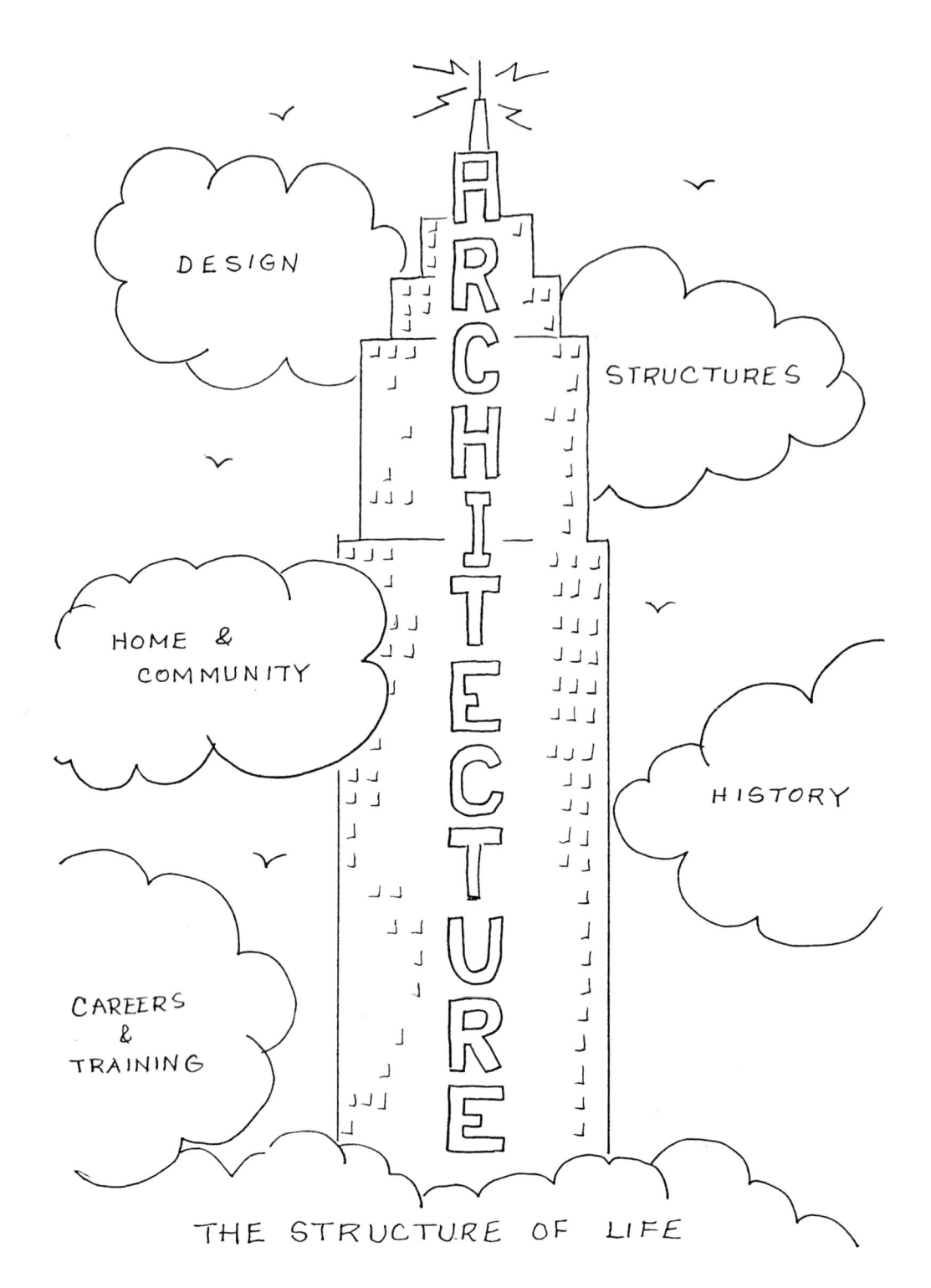

The Structure of Life

ARCHITECTURE

- DESIGN
- STRUCTURES
- HOME & COMMUNITY
- HISTORY
- CAREERS & TRAINING

THE STRUCTURE OF LIFE

Welcome to My World

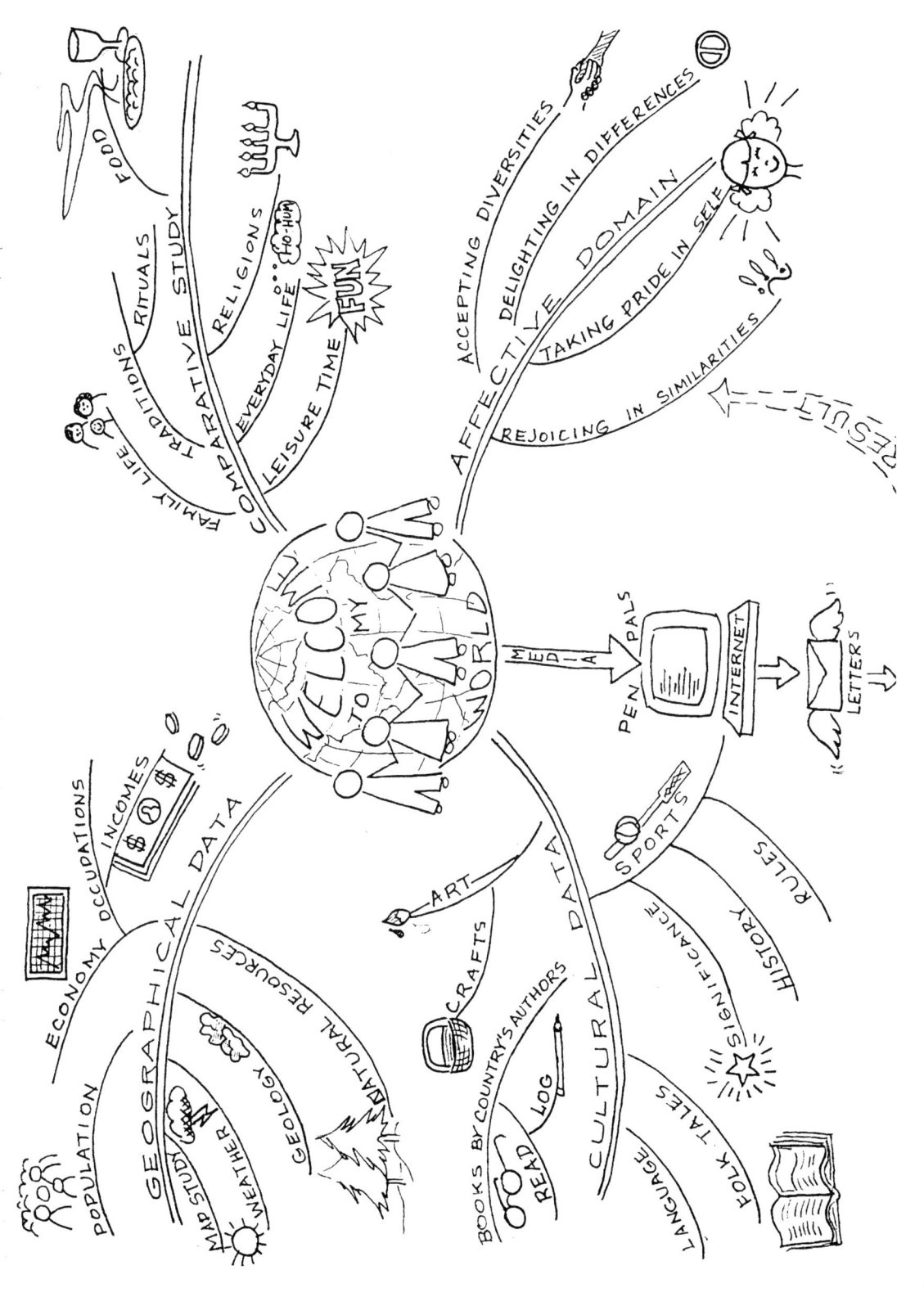

Welcome to My World

By Kathleen Mariko Yanamura

In many classrooms of today, students have instant access to what is happening in any part of the world via the Internet. Each day brings an expanding awareness of countries and cultures that may at first seem strange and exotic but actually have a variety of common denominators. Teachers with technology in their classrooms must accept the responsibility of helping students understand their global neighbors, so that their future will be a mutually beneficial one.

This unit is designed for contrasting the United States with another country through examination of the histories, languages, food, religions, geographies, literature, theater, music, and daily lives of the citizens of both countries. The activities may be adapted and modified by students to personalize the study to their interests and for designing their own projects as well. Students will also be able to work at their own pace in order to study a topic in as much depth and detail as they wish. Student interest and ownership is key to responsible learning.

Some activities allow students to examine their own education and construct or implement ways to improve it. Other activities ask for value judgments about health and physical well-being, leading students to make choices based on these judgments. Individual research, comparing and contrasting of cultures, creative writing, video production, and foreign language study provide enrichment to regular classroom curricula, so that students may immediately use their skills to the greatest extent.

Middle school students often do not embrace new peoples, cultures, or ideas easily. Exposure to other countries may help these students to accept others more willingly. Through this unit, therefore, it is anticipated that students will learn to appreciate the diversity of the people of Planet Earth, to delight in their differences, and to rejoice in their similarities, while taking pride in their own uniqueness.

Motivate

Lead a discussion on moving from a familiar place to somewhere totally different. What are the feelings of the "new kid in school"? How do these feelings change with time? How may students help the new student to adjust to change? How are the feelings of acceptance of a new student similar to those of learning about new and different cultures?

At this point, students will either decide on a country to be studied as a whole class or on specific countries they will individually research. If the study is focused on one country, they will then brainstorm a list of the things they already know about the country, as well as a list of things to research. If independent study is to be the focus, students will write what they already know about their selected countries in their journals, as well as what they wish to know.

As the unit progresses, new knowledge may be compared with previous perceptions. This will give students the opportunity to recognize differences or to verify accuracy.

Throughout the unit, a pen pal connection through the Internet and by regular mail will be used to motivate the study of the selected country.

Integrate

This unit integrates social studies, language arts, science, and computer science. Visual/spatial, intrapersonal, interpersonal, auditory/musical, logical/mathematical, bodily/kinesthetic, verbal/linguistic intelligences will be utilized throughout the unit.

Associate

Individual: research, journal writing, creative writing, learning centers, pen pals, book reports

Pair-Share: language practice, research projects, creative writing, crafts, drama

Small-Group: drama, cooperative learning, cooking, debate

Whole-Group: mind mapping, brainstorming, guest speakers, book talks, demonstrations, sharing final products with classmates, dramatic production, culture day, games, music, discussions

Activate

This unit is designed to provide a natural, essential, and very positive experience with using the resources of the library. It requires each student to know how to access materials, depending upon the country studied. The flexibility and resources are limitless.

Students should choose from the following activities. You may decide the number of projects to be completed by the whole class and by individual students. All projects will be prepared for presentation at a culture day exhibition. The following activities correlate with the social studies, science, and language arts curricula.

Listed after each activity are the method of association, the subjects integrated, and the intelligences used.

1. (a) Choose a specific city or town in the country you have selected. With a partner, research the location, geography, weather, geology, and economy of the area.
   Associate: pair-share
   Subjects: social studies, science
   Intelligences: interpersonal, verbal/linguistic

   (b) Make a chart comparing the geography, weather, geology, and economy of your town and that of the selected country.
   Associate: pair-share
   Subjects: social studies, science
   Intelligences: logical/mathematical, visual/spatial

2. Select a book written by an author from the country you have chosen. Keep an evaluation log of each chapter, with a sentence or two telling what you learned, felt,

appreciated, enjoyed, or disliked. Include comments about the story line and characters. See your teacher for a suggested book list.
Associate: individual
Subject: language arts
Intelligences: interpersonal

3. From a list provided by the teacher, choose a pen pal to write to throughout the unit.

LETTERS

Write once or twice a month, both by mail and through the Internet. Keep a log of the letters you have sent and received, with a sentence or two on your thoughts and reactions to the contents.
Associate: individual or pair-share
Subjects: language arts, computer science
Intelligences: interpersonal, intrapersonal, verbal/linguistic, visual/spatial

4. Brainstorm a list of questions to ask your pen pal about his or her school. After receiving a response, compare and contrast schools of the two countries, using the following questions as guides: Where would you rather go to school? Why? Where do you think you would get a better education? What makes one school system better than the other? Are there things about schools in that country that you would like to see happening at your school? How might they be implemented? Mind map information about the schools for the entire class. Be prepared to present this orally to classmates.
Associate: whole-group
Subjects: social studies, language arts
Intelligences: intrapersonal, verbal/linguistic, logical/mathematical

5. (a) Individually or with a partner, compare the diets of both countries. Highlight the ways diet affects the health and physical appearance of each group of people. Discuss the benefits and drawbacks to each diet and your food preferences. Present this information in a creative way.
Associate: independent or small-group
Subject: science
Intelligences: verbal/linguistic, visual/spatial

(b) Prepare a dish that might be part of a typical meal of the chosen country.
Associate: individual or pair-share
Subject: social studies
Intelligences: logical/mathematical

6. (a) With a group of three or four students, make a video showing a typical day at school. Introduce the principal, the secretary, some teachers, support staff, and students. Edit and narrate your video. After presenting it

first to the class, send it to a class in the country you are studying.
Associate: small-group
Subjects: language arts, social studies
Intelligences: visual/spatial

(b) Gather souvenirs from your town to be included in a care package to send with the video.
Associate: whole-group
Subject: social studies
Intelligences: interpersonal, visual/spatial

7. (a) Read some folktales from the two countries, noting similarities and differences, as well as the morals that the stories present. Write a story patterned after folktales from either of the cultures.
Associate: individual, whole-group
Subject: language arts
Intelligences: verbal/linguistic

(b) Create a folktale skit.
Associate: individual and small-group
Subjects: language arts, social studies
Intelligences: visual/spatial, verbal/linguistic

8. (a) Learn as much as you can about a ritual of significance in your chosen country, including the times and places that the ritual is performed and similar American rituals for presentation to the class. If possible, learn how to perform the ceremony and demonstrate it.
Associate: individual or pair-share
Subject: social studies
Intelligences: bodily/kinesthetic, visual/spatial, interpersonal, intrapersonal

(b) Research one of the country's holidays that is celebrated with special ceremonies; make a creative visual/spatial display.
Associate: individual
Subject: social studies
Intelligences: verbal/linguistic, visual/spatial

9. Interview a native of the country about his or her life there. Ask for a comparison of life in America with that of the person's previous homeland.
Associate: individual or pair-share
Subjects: language arts, social studies
Intelligences: interpersonal, verbal/linguistic

10. (a) With a partner, research the architectural styles of homes in the country you have chosen.
Associate: pair-share
Subject: social studies

Intelligences: verbal/linguistic

(b) Create a three-dimensional model of a home from that country. Include garden landscaping, as well as interior and exterior design. Keep a log of your work and research.
Associate: pair-share
Subject: social studies
Intelligences: bodily/kinesthetic, verbal/linguistic, interpersonal

11. (a) Research the history and significance of a sport of the country. Learn about the life of a sports hero and report what you have learned to the class.
Associate: individual or pair-share
Subjects: physical education, social studies
Intelligences: verbal/linguistic

(b) Set up a mock match for your classmates to experience. (You may or may not want to use traditional costumes or uniforms for this.)
Associate: individual or pair-share
Subjects: physical education, social studies
Intelligences: bodily/kinesthetic

12. Choose a craft from the chosen country, and then teach it to a partner or a small-group of students. Keep a log of your progress and feelings during the learning and teaching.
Associate: whole- or small-group
Subjects: art, language arts
Intelligences: bodily/kinesthetic, interpersonal

13. (a) Create a miniature garden in the style of your country's culture; make a creative display explaining your project.
Associate: individual
Subject: social studies
Intelligences: bodily/kinesthetic, visual/spatial

(b) Find out about the trees that are indigenous to the country you are studying. Focus on one species and create a booklet on it.
Associate: individual
Subjects: art, science, language arts
Intelligences: bodily/kinesthetic, visual/spatial

14. (a) Listen to tapes and practice speaking the language of your country. Make two 3" × 5" index cards for each new word learned—one with the English word at the top, the other with the word in the other language at the top. Add these to a class card file. Include the word's correct pronunciation and its translation.
Associate: individual, pair-share
Subject: language arts
Intelligences: verbal/linguistic, visual/spatial, interpersonal

(b) Some countries have more than one language. Make

charts showing translations for simple words and phrases in the language or languages of your country. Develop a creative way of listing some words using both the English translation and the foreign word.
Associate: individual, pair-share, small-group, or whole-group
Subject: language arts
Intelligences: bodily/kinesthetic, verbal/linguistic, visual/spatial

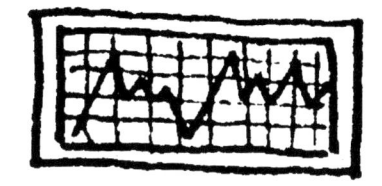

15. (a) As a class, research population densities, average incomes, and occupations in the United States and in the country you are studying. Create an interesting, creative graph that illustrates this information.
Associate: whole-group
Subject: math
Intelligences: visual/spatial, logical/mathematical

(b) Using the gathered information, brainstorm solutions to one of the following questions: What does this information tell you about life in that country? What are some of the problems you would face living in either country?
Associate: whole-group
Subject: social studies
Intelligences: logical

16. As a class, make a tape of some American songs. Write the words to these songs to send to your pen pal with a video or audiotape. Ask your pen pal to reciprocate.
Associate: whole-group
Subjects: auditory/music, language arts
Intelligences: musical, interpersonal

17. Add newly discovered information to a class wall chart that compares and contrasts American culture with the culture of the country you are studying.
Associate: whole-group
Subjects: language arts
Intelligences: interpersonal, intrapersonal

18. Explore family life in the selected country, noting similarities and differences in values taught in homes both here and there. Interview your pen pal about life outside of school to learn what your lives have in common and what is different. Present this information to the class.
Associate: individual
Subject: social studies
Intelligences: interpersonal, intrapersonal

19. Most cultures have dolls that are unique to that country. Find out the history and tradition behind a doll of the country

that you are studying. Make a doll of your own, or try to find one for display.
Associate: individual
Subject: social studies
Intelligences: bodily/
  kinesthetic, visual/spatial

20. (a) Tradition is very important in many countries. Ask your pen pal about some of his or her family's favorite traditions. Write a story about one of your own family's traditions and send it to your pen pal.
Associate: individual
Subjects: social studies, language arts
Intelligences: interpersonal, intrapersonal, verbal/linguistic

(b) Research the major religions of the country you are studying. Find out what part religion plays in the everyday lives of people in that country. Learn about the traditions that are a direct result of religious beliefs. Create a chart or write a paper that explains the basics of these religions.
Associate: individual
Subjects: social studies, language arts
Intelligences: verbal/linguistic, visual/spatial

21. As a class, research the history behind the economic strength or weakness of the country you are studying. Be prepared to participate in a discussion about the country's economy.
Associate: whole-group
Subject: social studies
Intelligences: interpersonal, verbal/linguistic

22. Design a map of the country that is large enough for display. Present a proposal to your teacher on the type of map you wish to draw and the information you intend to include on the map. Complete your project after it has been approved.
Associate: individual or pair-share
Subject: social studies
Intelligences: interpersonal, mathematical/logical, bodily/kinesthetic

Demonstrate
Portfolio Possibilities

While there are several options for evaluating the progress of the your students, you may choose to give grades based on criteria that you have set with students at the beginning of the unit. These criteria should include: quality, accuracy, creativity, and/or neatness.

1. Prior to the culture day presentation, have a parents' night for presenting projects and products created in the course of this unit.

2. Plan and execute a culture day for the entire school, focused on the country or countries studied by the group. All of the projects from this unit will be displayed, including research, stories, and student recipe booklets. Ethnic foods may be made available for tasting, and

crafts may be taught by students. Student videos may also be shown.

3. Produce a book of students' written reports for use as a reference for other students.

4. Perform a folktale or story of the chosen country in traditional theater form.

5. Prepare ethnic dishes for a luncheon. Compile a cookbook of recipes from both countries.

Communicate

1. Have students write thank you notes to guest speakers, individually, about what was learned or what was presented.

2. Invite students to act as guides for family night and culture day.

3. Have students design and distribute banners, posters, and flyers to advertise the exhibition in both the community and the school.

4. Help students place videos and the books they have written in the school library for checkout.

5. Contact local television, radio, and newspapers to cover the exhibition. Have students write media releases.

6. Encourage students to read created folktales to other classes and to place them in the library for checkout.

References

Prentice, M. *Catch Them Learning; A Handbook of Classroom Strategies*. Palatine, IL: IRI/Skylight Publishing, Inc., 1994.

My Country

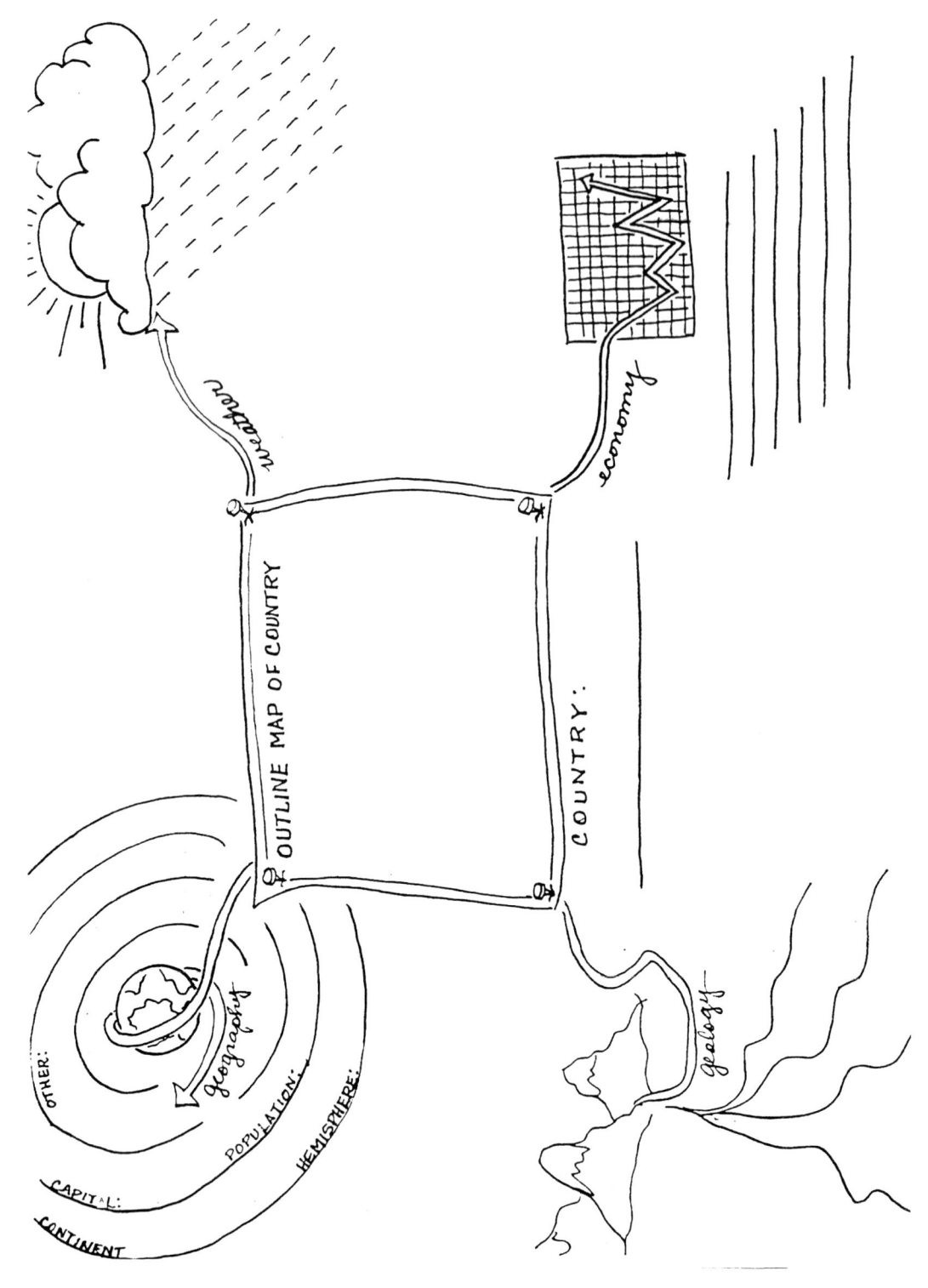

weather

economy

OUTLINE MAP OF COUNTRY

COUNTRY:

geography

geology

OTHER:
POPULATION:
HEMISPHERE:
CAPITAL:
CONTINENT

Holidays

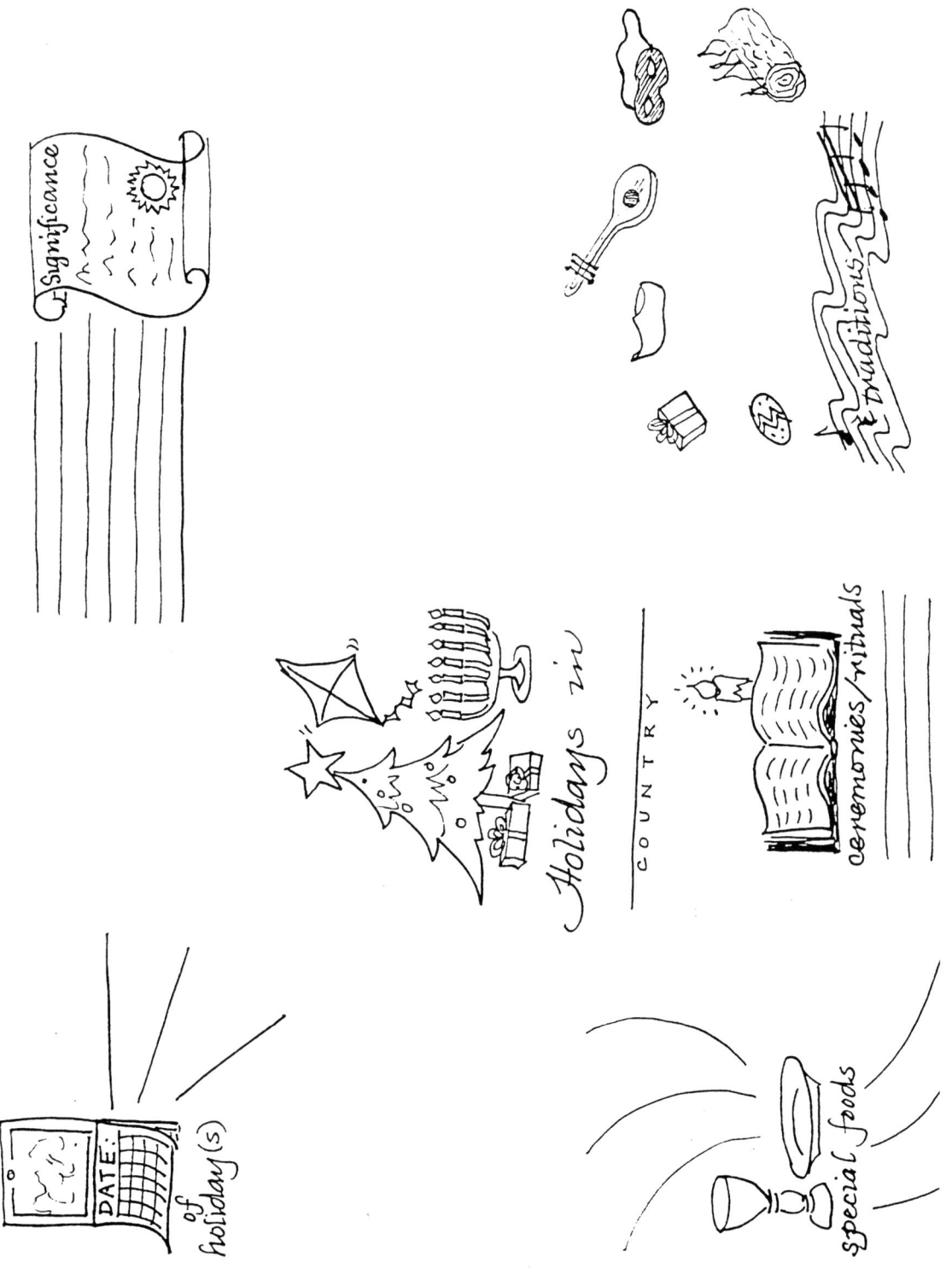

Sports

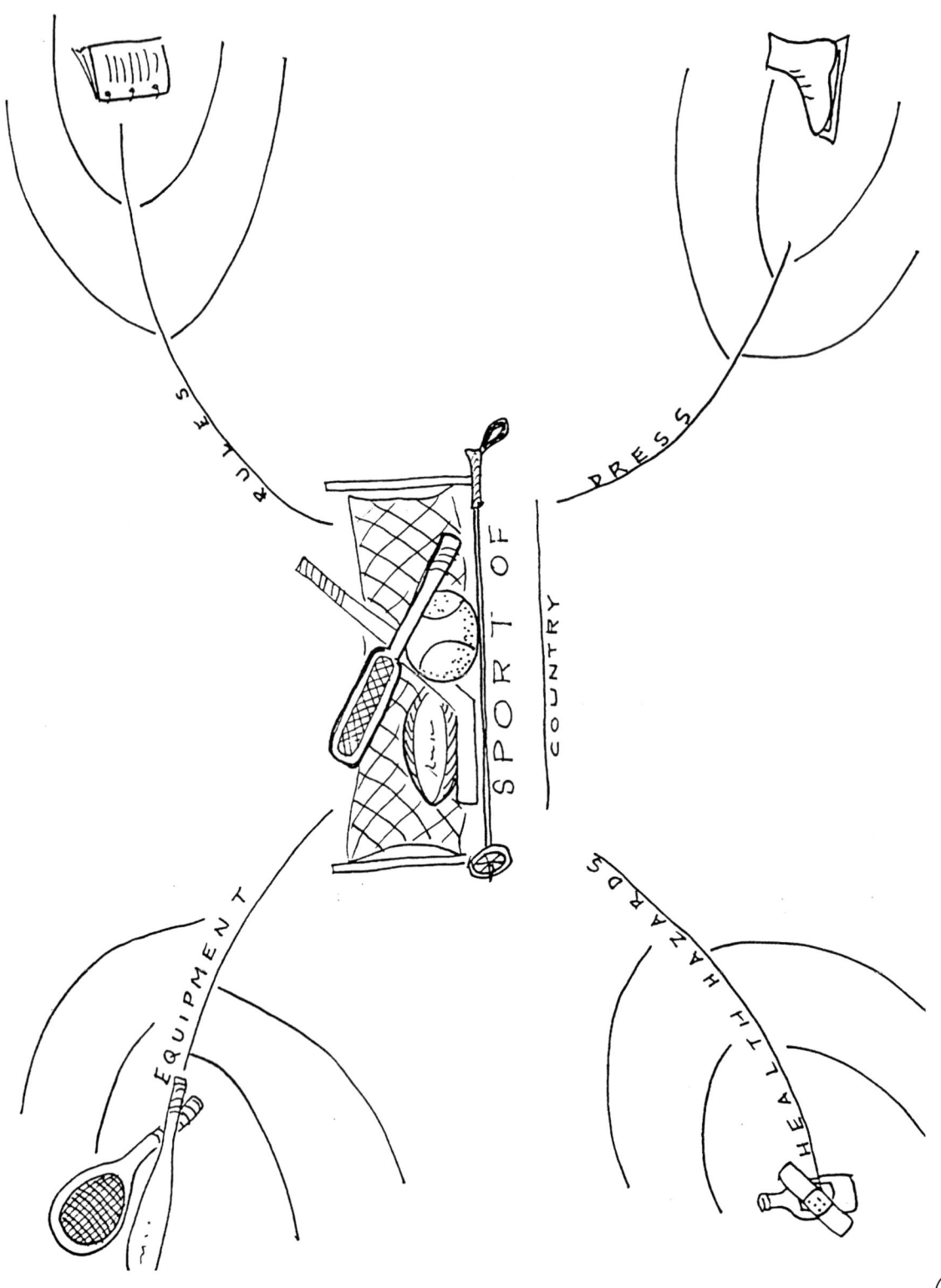

The Great Depression

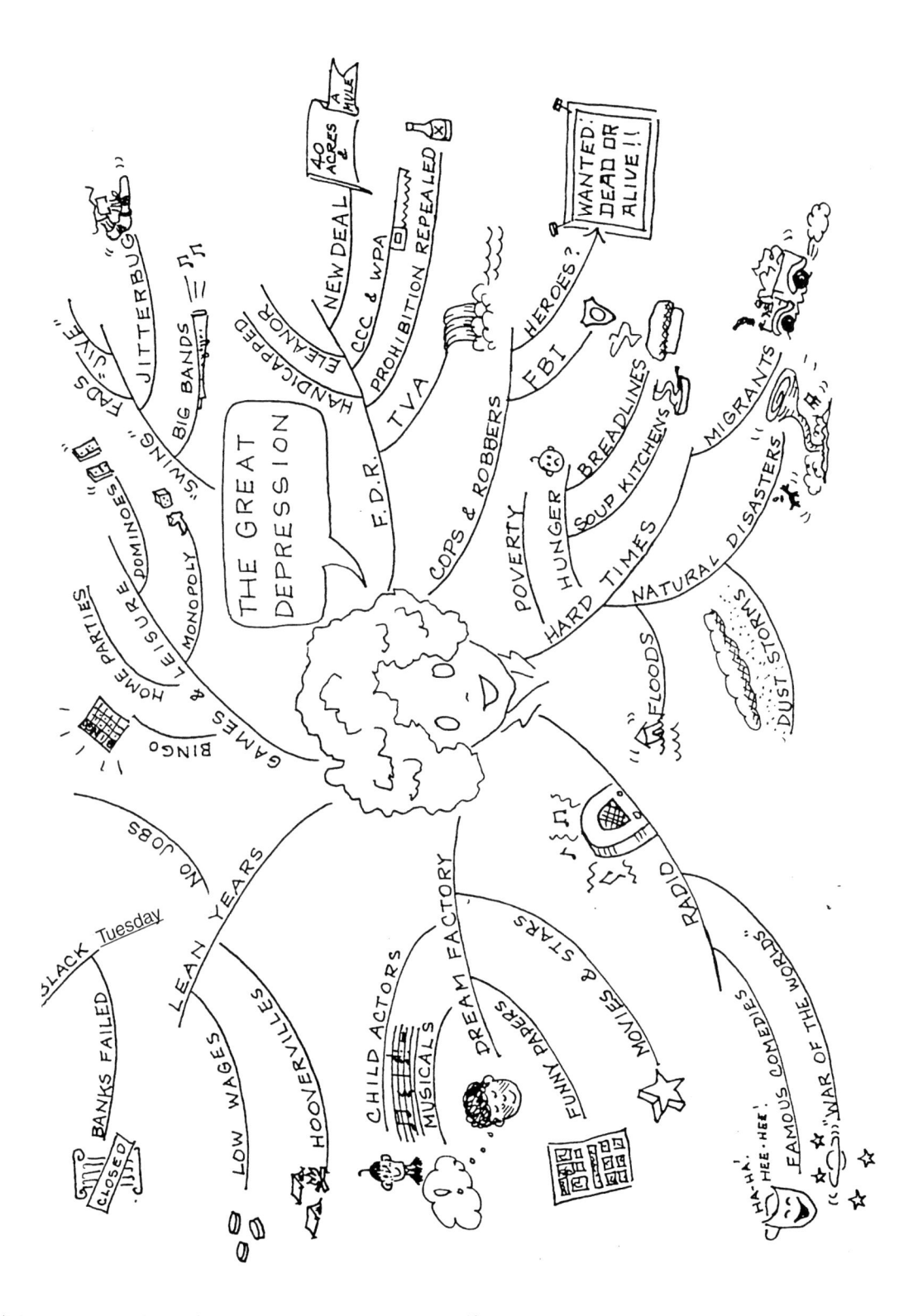

The Great Depression

By Judith Bynum

In the years separating the present time in history from the period known as the Great Depression, this country went through World War II, a conflict called the Cold War, a war in Korea, a war in Vietnam, and a televised war in the Persian Gulf. Nine presidents have been in the White House. Entire world governments have risen and fallen. And incredible growth has occurred, both in technology and social change. To most Americans, the story of the Depression is so far removed from our world today that it is difficult to understand. There remains a sense of connection however, between the Depression and the present. Much of this connection can be attributed to the stories still told by so many people who lived through the Depression and carry memories of it with them (Watkins, 1993). These oral traditions have become part of the common heritage of many families.

Students who experience these stories vicariously can find a measure of pride in the durability and character of the men and women who survived that world of poverty and hunger. It was the "worst of times, a terrible scarring experience" that changed how people lived from that day on (Watkins, 1993). If children of today learn to appreciate the hard times of their ancestors, they may better bridge the generation gap. Perhaps if this generation does learn about the past from their grandparents and great-grandparents, an economic disaster like the Great Depression may not happen again.

For classes that cannot spend an extended amount of time on this unit, there are two options:

1. Students may be divided into eight groups, with each group focusing on one specific section. Through researching and participating in the suggested activities related to that topic, student groups will learn about the Depression, and then teach what they have learned to the whole class through creative presentations.

2. You may select from the activities in each area, personalizing the unit for your class.

Motivate

Show students the movie *The Grapes of Wrath,* and have them list visual characteristics of the people and the times depicted. Lead a brainstorming exercise on what students already know about the Depression. Have students interview senior citizens who lived during the Depression or relate a story that has been passed down by a member of their own family who lived during that era.

Integrate

This unit integrates social studies, math and language arts. Auditory/musical, bodily/kinesthetic, logical/mathematical, verbal/linguistic, visual/spatial, interpersonal, and intrapersonal intelligences will be addressed throughout the unit.

Associate

In the following exercises, students will work independently in interviewing subjects and doing other forms of research. Small groups will be formed for the purposes of games and simulations. The class as a whole will watch movies, listen to guest speaker presentations, and participate in discussions.

Activate

Students will choose at least one activity from each numbered section. Starred activities may be conducted by the whole class.

1. **Journey Through the Lean Years**

    (a) Compare the average annual earnings of workers in the 1930's with those of workers in the same careers today. Compute the percentage of increase. Make a visual display of the data you have collected.
    Associate: small-group
    Subject: math
    Intelligences: mathematical/logical

    (b) Research Hoovervilles and define the following terms: Hoover blankets, Hoover flags, Hoover hogs, Hoover wagons. Present your research creatively to the class.
    Associate: small-group
    Subject: language arts
    Intelligences: verbal, interpersonal

    (c) Research Black Tuesday and present your findings to the class.
    Associate: independent
    Subject: social studies
    Intelligences: verbal

    (d) Compare the costs of items now and in the 1930's, using the "Depression Shopping List: 1932 to 1934" (Edey, 1969). Spend $1,000, now and then. Make a poster of comparisons to show to the class.
    Associate: small-group
    Subject: math
    Intelligences: logical/mathematical

2. **Dream Factory**

    *(a) Watch the video of *Annie.* In small groups, discuss visual clues of conditions during the

Depression for both the wealthy and the poor. Research important persons and places noted in the video. Report your findings to the class.
Associate: whole-group, independent
Subject: language arts
Intelligences: visual, verbal, musical

*(b) The funny papers became an important part of life for children during the Depression. The characters in *Little Orphan Annie, Flash Gordon, Tarzan, Tom Mix, Buck Rogers,* and *Dick Tracy* were heroes and heroines to many children in this era. Find examples of these characters in books, movies, or toys, and share your findings with the class.
Associate: whole-group
Subject: language arts
Intelligences: bodily/kinesthetic, visual/spatial

*(c) Child stars of the movies and children of famous people were in the news during the 1930's. Shirley Temple was a famous child star of that time. The young princesses, Elizabeth and Margaret Rose Windsor, whose father was crowned king of England in 1937, were the subjects of storybooks and paper dolls. The Little Rascals were popular with children also. A sad occurrence during this time period was the kidnapping of the Lindbergh baby. In groups, plan a lesson for the class on one of these topics, including visual/spatial aids.
Associate: small-group
Subjects: language arts; social studies
Intelligences: visual/spatial, verbal/linguistic

*(d) Watch a Shirley Temple movie and a Little Rascals film. Discuss the purpose of these movies during the Depression years.
Associate: whole-group
Subjects: language arts, social studies
Intelligences: visual/spatial, auditory/musical

*(e) Many movie stars of the 1930's are still famous today. List something that you know about the following stars: Fred Astaire and Ginger Rogers; Nelson Eddy and Jeanette MacDonald; Snow White and the Seven Dwarfs; Clark Gable; Bette Davis; Mickey Rooney; Judy Garland; James Cagney; W. C. Fields; King Kong; Errol Flynn; Alfred Hitchcock; Humphrey Bogart; KatharineHepburn. If some of the names in this list are unfamiliar, ask a senior citizen to help you identify them.
Associate: whole-group
Subject: social studies

Intelligences: verbal/linguistic, interpersonal

3. **Hard Times**

   (a) Poverty became a part of everyone's life during the Depression. Through interviews and research, explore the impact of the Depression on one of the following groups of people: factory workers, single men, farmers, businessmen. Write an essay comparing the Depression's toll on their lives.
   Associate: independent
   Subjects: language arts, social studies
   Intelligences: verbal/linguistic, interpersonal

   (b) Breadlines and soup kitchens became part of the normal way of life in cities during the Depression. Plan a bread-and-soup meal for the class; have each classmate bring one vegetable for the soup, or some bread.
   Associate: whole-group
   Subject: social studies
   Intelligences: bodily/kinesthetic

   (c) During the 1930's, dust storms and floods devastated some farmers. Find stories about people who survived these natural disasters or research specific natural disasters that occurred at that time, such as the Flood of 1936 or the dust storms in the Dust Bowl area of Texas. Make a diorama of the event.
   Associate: independent
   Subjects: social studies, language arts
   Intelligences: visual/spatial, verbal/linguistic

   (d) Pretend you are hungry and must stand in a breadline or eat at a soup kitchen in order to survive. It is winter, and you have no coat. Your mother is sick, and you must stay home from school to care for her. Your father has gone away to find work, but your family has gotten no letters or money from him since he left. Write a story about your feelings, your hopes, and your fears.
   Associate: independent
   Subjects: social studies, language arts
   Intelligences: intrapersonal, verbal/linguistic

4. **Radio**

   *(a) Listen to a cassette recording of famous radio broadcasts of comedy serials, such as the *Jack Benny Show*. Discuss how the class pictured the characters. Would it have been (was it) better on television? Why or why not? Write your opinions in your journal.
   Associate: whole-group
   Subject: language arts
   Intelligences: verbal/linguistic, auditory/musical

   *(b) Among the memorable radio programs was one that began as a Halloween joke but wound up scaring the nation half to death. The story simulated news broadcasts

announcing that invasion forces from Mars had landed in New Jersey and were devastating the countryside with death rays. America panicked. Choose parts and read "War of the Worlds." Discuss the panic it caused at the time of its original broadcast. Do you think something similar could happen in your lifetime? Why or why not?
Associate: whole-group
Subject: language arts
Intelligences: verbal/linguistic, bodily/kinesthetic

(c) Bring pictures of old radios to class. Research the history of radios and the changes that have occurred in their technology and design over the years.
Associate: independent
Subject: social studies
Intelligences: verbal/linguistic, visual/spatial

(d) Visit a local radio station to learn about programming. Write and produce a radio show, complete with sound effects and music.
Associate: small-group or whole-group
Subject: social studies
Intelligences: auditory/musical, verbal/linguistic

5. **Cops and Robbers**

(a) While businesses of the 1930's closed and farms lay barren, an alarming number of Americans began looking for easy money through robbery, kidnapping, and murder. Choose one of the following to discuss with the class: Bonnie Parker and Clyde Barrow, Bruno Richard Hauptmann, John Dillinger, "Pretty Boy" Floyd, or "Ma" Barker and Her Boys. Memories from senior citizens will be especially interesting.
Associate: independent or small-group
Subject: social studies
Intelligences: verbal/linguistic

(b) J. Edgar Hoover was the head of the FBI during the Depression. Write to the FBI for information and draw a mind map outlining the agency's purpose or research Hoover, drawing a poster showing his accomplishments.
Associate: independent
Subject: social studies
Intelligences: verbal/linguistic, visual/spatial

*(c) Watch a cops-and-robbers movie from the 1930's. Compare the black-and-white medium with color in the "feel" of the movie. Cite differences in movies about law enforcement then and now. Which do you prefer and why? Write your thoughts in your journal.
Associate: whole-group
Subject: language arts
Intelligences: visual/spatial, verbal/linguistic, intrapersonal

*(d) Some movies about cops and robbers made heroes of the

lawbreakers, and others made heroes of the law enforcers. Give examples of each and discuss how the movie's point of view affects feelings about the characters.
Associate: whole-group
Subjects: language arts, social studies
Intelligences: verbal/linguistic, interpersonal

6. **F.D.R.**

   *(a) When Franklin D. Roosevelt became the thirty-second President of the United States, the country was scared. Roosevelt immediately began working on ending the Depression through a series of programs and changes. Break into small groups and choose one topic from the following list. Research your topic as a group, and present your findings to the entire class.
   Topics: the Tennessee Valley Authority; Prohibition; CCC and WPA; the New Deal.
   Associate: small-group
   Subject: social studies
   Intelligences: verbal/linguistic, logical/mathematical

   (b) List Roosevelt's outstanding characteristics. What were his handicaps and how did he overcome them? Write an essay on a person you know who overcame a handicap during his or her lifetime.
   Associate: independent
   Subject: social studies
   Intelligences: verbal/linguistic, interpersonal

   (c) Eleanor Roosevelt played an important role in her husband's presidency. Read her biography and creatively present your findings to the class.
   Associate: independent
   Subject: social studies
   Intelligences: verbal/linguistic

   (d) Draw a family tree of Theodore Roosevelt and Franklin Roosevelt's family to show the two men's relationship.
   Associate: small-group or independent
   Subject: social studies
   Intelligences: logical/mathematical

7. **Swing**

   *(a) Listen to the music of the big bands, such as Benny Goodman, Tommy Dorsey, Glenn Miller, or Duke Ellington. Learn simple steps of the jitterbug. Why did many parents think it was a "bad" dance?
   Associate: whole-group
   Subject: social studies
   Intelligences: auditory/musical, bodily/kinesthetic

   (b) Learn some songs of the 1930's and teach them to your classmates.
   Associate: whole-group
   Subject: social studies
   Intelligences: auditory/musical

   (c) Study fads and styles of the 1930's and today. Prepare an oral presentation with visual/spatials to present to the class.
   Associate: independent or

small-group
Subject: social studies
Intelligences: verbal/linguistic, visual/spatial

(d) Learn jive talk
Associate: whole-group
Subjects: social studies, language arts
Intelligences: verbal/linguistic

8. **Games and Leisure**

*(a) During the Depression, people stayed home and played games instead of going out for entertainment. Monopoly became a favorite game, as did dominoes and bingo. Hold a Monopoly tournament with creative prizes of the Depression (an old shoe, a bowl of dust, and other creative wordplay items).

Associate: whole-group
Subject: social studies
Intelligences: bodily/kinesthetic

(b) Play other games of the Depression.
Associate: small-group
Subject: social studies
Intelligences: bodily/kinesthetic, logical/mathematical

(c) Create a bingo game with people, places, and things of the 1930's, instead of numbers.
Associate: small-group
Subject: social studies
Intelligences: verbal/linguistic, logical/mathematical

(d) Create a Monopoly-type game based on your own community.
Associate: small-group
Subjects: social studies, language arts
Intelligences: verbal/linguistic, logical/mathematical

(e) During the Depression, families in rural areas met once a month for entertainment. At their meetings, they presented songs, readings, musical numbers, or stories. Plan a talent show in which members of the class may participate.
Associate: whole-group
Subject: social studies
Intelligences: bodily/kinesthetic, verbal/linguistic, auditory/musical

Demonstrate

Portfolio Possibilities

Select three of the following activities, with your instructor's approval.

1. Plan and hold a funny-papers day. Create funny-papers character costumes for yourselves or dolls. Videotape the event.
   Associate: whole-group
   Subject: language arts
   Intelligences: bodily/kinesthetic, interpersonal

2. Have a soup-and-bread lunch. Serve soup to the cafeteria

workers.
Associate: whole-group
Subject: social studies
Intelligences: bodily/kinesthetic, interpersonal

3. Plan and execute a radio program with a Roosevelt-style fireside chat, a comedy, music of the era, and commercials of the times. Present your program to other classes.
Associate: whole-group or small-group
Subjects: social studies, language arts
Intelligences: bodily/kinesthetic, verbal/linguistic

4. Create games with 1930's themes. Have a game day to share your games with other students.
Associate: whole-group or small-group
Subjects: language arts, math
Intelligences: bodily/kinesthetic, visual/spatial, verbal/linguistic, interpersonal

5. How, when, where, why? Draw mind maps of the Depression years to evaluate the unit. The maps will be used to teach others.
Associate: whole-group
Subject: social studies
Intelligences: visual/spatial, intrapersonal

6. Discuss reasons that wartime is good for the economy. How did World War II help end the Depression?
Associate: whole-group
Subject: social studies
Intelligences: visual/spatial, intrapersonal

7. In the 1930's, recycling was a way of life. Brainstorm uses for a sack of flour, a pair of overalls, and a kernel of corn. If your campus doesn't have a recycling strategy, plan one and implement it.
Associate: whole and small-group
Subject: social studies
Intelligences: bodily/kinesthetic, verbal/linguistic

8. Write a paper explaining the causes of the Great Depression and the ways in which it changed the shape of our government.
Associate: independent
Subject: social studies
Intelligences: verbal/linguistic

Communicate

1. Teach another class about the Depression, addressing all learning modalities.
Associate: whole-group or small-group
Subject: social studies
Intelligences: visual/spatial, verbal/linguistic, bodily/kinesthetic

2. Invite senior citizens to come to class to talk about the Depression. With their permission, make videotapes of the visitors during their talks.
Associate: whole-group
Subject: social studies
Intelligences: interpersonal, visual/spatial, auditory/musical

3. Compile a booklet of interview stories for distribution to local school and town libraries and museums. Give taped interviews to the museum archives, as well.
Associate: whole-group
Subjects: language arts, social studies
Intelligences: interpersonal, verbal/linguistic

4. Write news releases for a local newspaper concerning your recycling project and its success.

Associate: independent
Subject: language arts
Intelligences: verbal/linguistic

References

Donovan, H., ed. *New Deal and War. Vol. 11: 1933–1945: The Life History of the United States.* New York: Time-Life Books, 1964.

Edey, M., ed. *This Fabulous Century: 1930–1940.* Morristown, NJ: Time-Life Books, 1969.

Fibber McGee and Molly: *The Original Broadcasts from Radio's Golden Age.* New Rochelle, NY: Great American Audio.

Judd, D., producer. *Split Infinity: A Gift from the Past.* Murray, UT: Feature Films for Families.

Prentice, M. *Catch Them Learning: A Handbook of Classroom Strategies.* Palatine, IL: IRI/Skylight Publishing, Inc., 1994.

Steinbeck, J. *The Grapes of Wrath.* Livonia, MI: CBS/Fox Video, 1940.

Watkins, T. *The Great Depression: America in the 1930's.* Boston: Little, Brown, and Company, 1993.

What Are These Items?

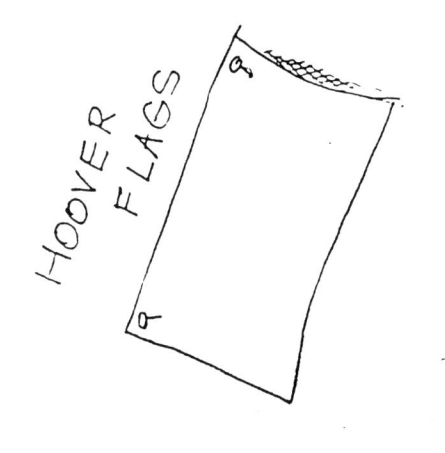

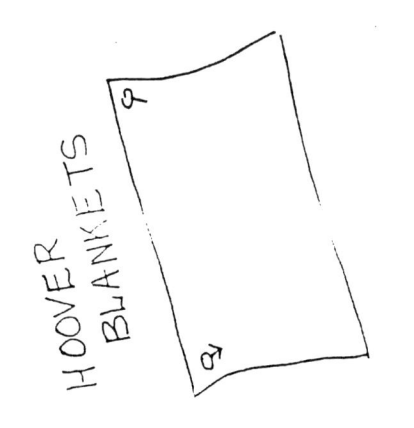

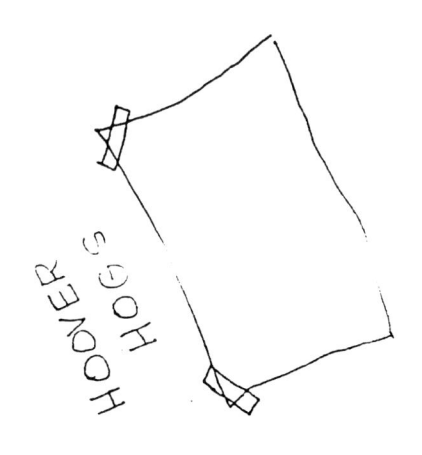

- HOOVER FLAGS
- HOOVER WAGONS
- HOOVERVILLE
- HOOVER BLANKETS
- HOOVER HOGS

What are these items?

Change

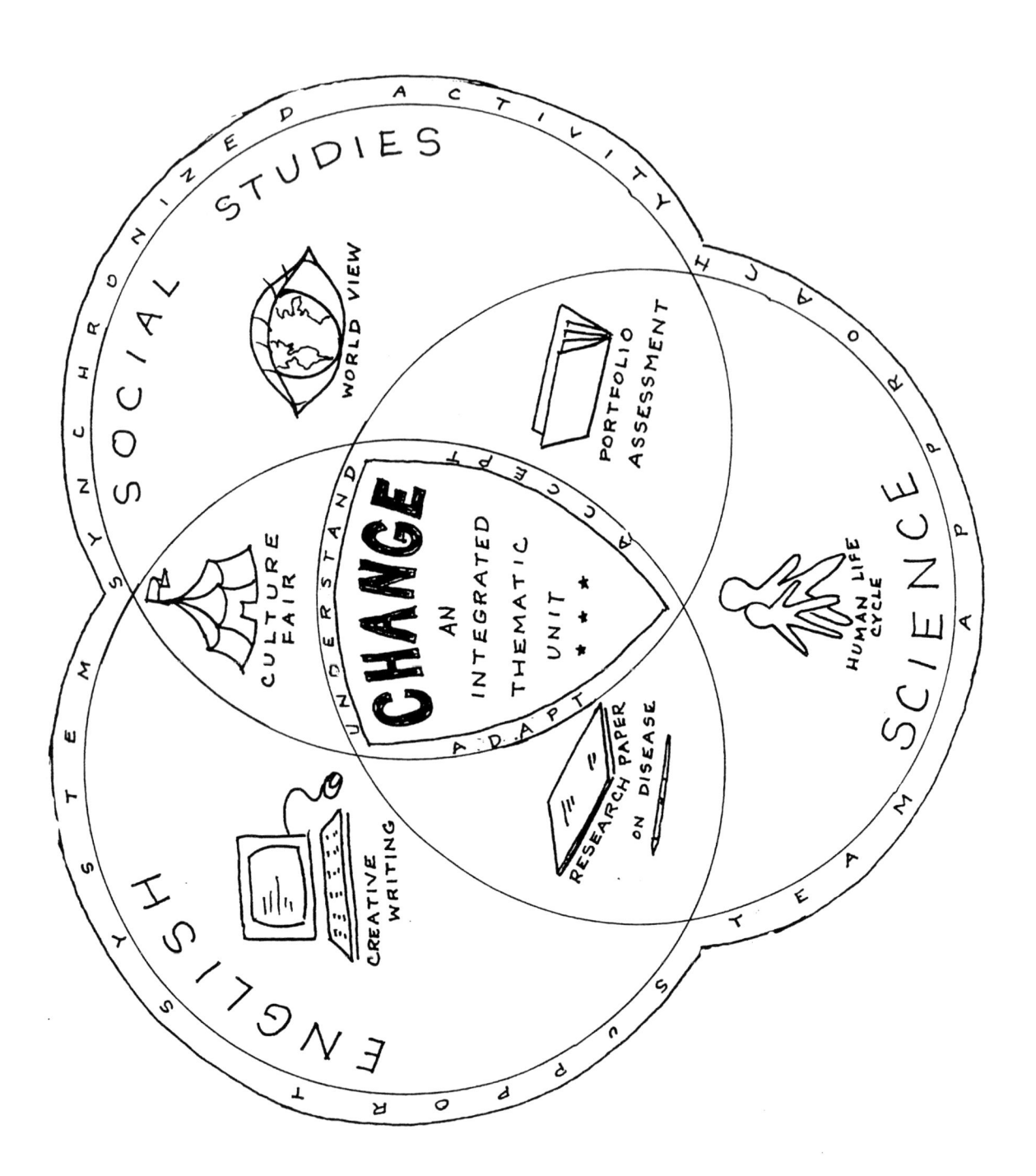

SOCIAL STUDIES — SYNCHRONIZED ACTIVITY
SCIENCE — HUMOR APPRAISAL TEAM
ENGLISH — SUPPORT SYSTEMS

- World View
- Portfolio Assessment
- Culture Fair
- Human Life Cycle
- Creative Writing
- Research Paper on Disease

CHANGE — An Integrated Thematic Unit

Understand · Accept · Adapt

©1997 J. Weston Walch, Publisher 80 *The Preadolescent*

Change

By Helen Hughes, Cindy Middleton, and Edna Yancey

There is more than one way to collaborate successfully. Many curriculum issues come into play in determining which collaboration methods are most compatible with your school. There are many benefits to writing integrated curriculum as a team. Teachers who write together multiply and reinforce the value of a selected topic. Team writing helps to establish a support system and an invaluable timesaving framework, as each individual member can contribute his or her talents during the development of curricular activities. The synchronization of these activities in each content area conserves both teacher instruction and student learning time. Parents react positively when they see teachers working as a team. Sharing in the celebration of various students' demonstrations of learning such as the culture fair in this unit, encourages communication between parents and students. By becoming participants instead of traditional observers, parents recognize the value of thematic instruction and support team endeavors.

In this unit, teachers present the theme of "change" holistically by integrating the subjects of science, social studies, and English. This team approach requires curricular modification in content, and timing becomes a critical factor. A spirit of cooperation and flexibility is needed to ensure the unit's success.

In the midst of their own personal kaleidoscope, it is sometimes hard for preadolescents to understand, accept, or adapt to the changes in themselves and the in the world around them. The ultimate aim of any middle school team of teachers is to give preadolescents an across- the-curriculum world view of the concept of change. It is hoped that students will acquire a personal reference of how change affects their lives, their futures, and the ones they love and will love.

The goals of this unit are:

1. To develop students' understanding of the human life cycle and how each stage of development offers opportunities to grow intellectually, socially, and emotionally.

2. To create an understanding of the vast governmental, cultural, and economic changes taking place in Central and South America and to appreciate how such changes inevitably affect the United States.

3. To help students develop effective writing skills that will assist them in productively dealing with the rapidly changing world around them.

Motivate

The following activities need to be conducted on the same day if at all possible. Preadolescents will transfer a concept more easily from one discipline to another if it is presented within a condensed time frame. This approach provides a frame of reference that can be retrieved intermittently throughout the unit.

In science class, students will bring one of their baby pictures to class. The pictures will be numbered and placed on the walls of the room. The students will try to determine which picture belongs to which student. They will be asked to take notes on how they arrived at their conclusions. A discussion will follow on how life is a process of change from the moment of conception until death.

In social studies, students will brainstorm answers to the following question: If America were no longer a democracy but a dictatorship, what changes might occur in your family life, your social life, the economic system, and the school system? A discussion will follow on the impact upon a country's people in every area of life when drastic governmental changes are made.

In English class, the teacher will draw three intertwining circles on the board. The first circle will be labeled "You," the second "Community," and the third, "The World." The students will brainstorm the changes they have seen in these three areas of their lives in the past five years. The teacher will then ask the students to visualize future changes by writing a composition entitled "In the Year A.D. 2050." The students will read their compositions to the class.

Integrate

Although this unit is written for three content areas, it can be easily adapted to dual combinations, such as social studies/English or science/English. Math could be incorporated if the team consists of four content area teachers.

The unit infuses the concept of "change" in each content base: science, social studies, and English.

Associate

Each content area should provide a variety of grouping forms during the unit. Team members should discuss the importance of particular groupings for specific activities. In other words, each activity needs to elicit an appropriate grouping.

Whole groups, small groups, and individual endeavors are interwoven throughout the unit in each of the subject areas.

Activate

There are three critical concerns for the team in this component of curriculum writing. First, when generating activities, provision for the various learning styles is a necessity in each content area. Second, if it is not possible to provide for the seven intelligences in all three subjects, then one content area should be selected by team members as the one most conducive to providing for them. For instance, in this unit, social studies emerges as the predominant discipline that could readily utilize and develop activities for the seven intelligences. Third, timing becomes a critical factor for the activities. The individual team members must have a constant open dialogue among themselves on the progress of daily activities in the classroom.

Activities

Science

1. Discuss the five different levels of organization in all living things (cells, tissues, organs, organ systems, organisms).
   Associate: whole-group
   Subject: science
   Intelligences: verbal/linguistic

2. Make posters of the four stages of mitosis, showing the changes taking place from prophase to metaphase to anaphase to telophase.
   Associate: individual
   Subject: science
   Intelligences: bodily/kinesthetic

3. View a filmstrip entitled, *Stages of Life: Reproduction, Growth, and Change.* Follow the film with a class discussion on the reproductive process.
   Associate: whole-group
   Subject: science
   Intelligences: visual/spatial, verbal/linguistic

4. Have students break into groups of four and create an imaginary story based on the process of reproduction, beginning with the sperm and egg and ending with birth. The story must contain dialogue between the egg and sperm and/or between the newborn's thoughts and the comments of the doctors, nurses, or parent(s) at the time of delivery. Each group will present their stories to the class.
   Associate: small-group
   Subject: science
   Intelligences: verbal/linguistic, interpersonal

5. Present the video *The Miracle of Life.* Following the video, discuss the birth process with students.
   Associate: whole-group
   Subject: science
   Intelligences: visual/spatial, verbal/linguistic

6. Discuss the four stages of development and the changes that occur after birth (infancy, childhood, adolescence, and adulthood).
   Associate: whole-group
   Subject: science
   Intelligences: verbal/linguistic

7. Have students interview their parents on the students' life events, such as their age of grabbing at objects, sitting up, crawling, or talking. Ask them also to obtain information on growth, such as their first teeth or first steps, and share their findings with the class.
   Associate: individual
   Subject: science
   Intelligences: verbal/linguistic, intrapersonal

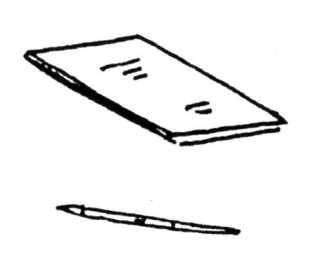

8. Present information on how diseases diminish our bodily functions, productivity, and life enjoyment at any developmental stage. Encourage students to share their personal or family experiences with certain diseases and discuss how illness has affected their lives.
Associate: whole-group
Subject: science
Intelligences: verbal/linguistic, intrapersonal

9. Present the video *Time Out: The Truth About HIV, AIDS, and You.* Follow it with a class discussion on how this twenty-first century disease will in one way or another affect all of the class.
Associate: whole-group
Subject: science
Intelligences: visual/spatial verbal/linguistic

Social Studies

1. Present the video *Mexico,* from Rand McNally. Follow it with a class discussion on the changes in this Latin American country since the Revolution of 1910. Special emphasis will be placed on Mexico City's vast economic growth.
Associate: whole-group
Subject: social studies
Intelligences: visual/spatial, verbal/linguistic

2. Present information on cultural changes brought about by the Revolution of 1910, especially in the areas of the arts and recreation in Mexico. Students, either in small groups or pairs, will choose from one of the following categories: music, painting, drama, games, or dance. They will find an example of one twentieth-century Mexican work in their category and present their art form or recreational activity to the class.
Associate: small-groups or pair-share
Subject: social studies
Intelligences: bodily/kinesthetic, auditory/musical, interpersonal

3. Find and share with the class one newspaper article concerning either the country of Haiti or Cuba. After your presentation, lead a class discussion on the leadership problems and changes in both countries, and how these changes have affected the economy and culture of the United States.
Associate: individual
Subject: social studies
Intelligences: visual/spatial, verbal/linguistic

4. Divide the class into into two groups. Assign the groups the Panama Canal issue (should the United States relinquish ownership in the year 2000 to the Panamanians?) or the Puerto Rico statehood issue (should this island become the fifty-first state of the United States?). Group members will decide which side of the issue they will defend. In a forum-style debate, each group will present both sides of the issues.

Associate: small-group
Subject: social studies
Intelligences: logical/mathematical, verbal/linguistic, interpersonal

5. Have students draw the Central American or Caribbean flag of their choice. They will present their flags to the class and discuss the meaning of the colors and symbols.
Associate: individual
Subject: social studies
Intelligences: visual/spatial, bodily/kinesthetic, verbal/linguistic

6. Present the video *Amazon, Land of Flooded Forest,* from *National Geographic.* Follow it with a class discussion on South American countries and the important places therein.
Associate: whole-group
Subject: social studies
Intelligences: visual/spatial, verbal/linguistic

7. Present brochures from different Latin American embassies to the class. Lead students in a discussion of the similarities and differences in the information presented in the different brochures.
Associate: whole-group
Subject: social studies
Intelligences: visual/spatial, verbal/linguistic

8. In pairs, the students will write questions for an upcoming panel of adults who have lived in either Central or South America. Some of the questions they construct must revolve around the concept of changes in the countries' economic structures, cultures, religions, industries, types of government, etc. Students will then interview the Latin American panel.
Associate: pair-share
Subject: social studies
Intelligences: verbal/linguistic, interpersonal

9. In a forum-style panel, the class will debate the issue, Should the rain forest be preserved or destroyed?
Associate: whole-group
Subject: social studies
Intelligences: logical/mathematical, verbal/linguistic

10. Give students a list of individuals who have made changes in Latin America. Ask them to choose someone from the list to research and write a report on. The English instructor will assist them in their writing. Have students present their finished reports to the class.
Associate: individual
Subjects: English, social studies
Intelligences: verbal/linguistic

English

1. Introduce the concept that writing is a constantly changing process which is never perfected. Place emphasis on how writing is now easier and faster than it was in the past, due to technological advances in computer word processing programs. If possible, have students experiment with a basic word processing program such as Microsoft Write.

Associate: individual
Subject: English
Intelligences: bodily/kinesthetic

2. Give students 10 basic skeletal sentences with the noun-verb-noun structure. An example might be, *Dogs chase cats.* Have students break into pairs and add words to make the sentences more meaningful and colorful. They will share their new sentences with the class.
Associate: pair-share
Subject: English
Intelligences: verbal/linguistic

3. Have students choose from one of the following types of paragraphs: narrative, descriptive, expository, and persuasive. They will write a paragraph on a topic of their own interest and share it with the class. Then ask them the following questions: Who was your audience? Would you have written differently for another audience? A discussion will follow on how writing for different audiences and purposes demands different styles of writing—for example, writing a letter to a friend versus writing reports for science or social studies.
Associate: individual
Subject: English
Intelligences: verbal/linguistic

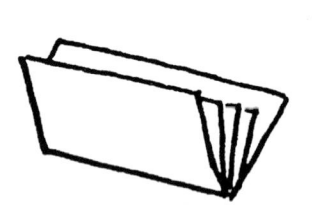

4. In preparation for their imaginative story in science involving the sperm and egg, have students choose their favorite animal and give it a name. With a partner, they will write a dialogue between their animal and their partner's animal. They must create a place and time for their conversation. An example might be: A bear named Lucy meets a cat named Penny at the mall on a Saturday morning. Students will present their conversations to the class.
Associate: pair-share
Subject: English
Intelligences: verbal/linguistic

5. Have students read and discuss the following two legends: "Popocatepetl and Ixtaccihuatl," by Juliet Piggott (from Mexico), and "The Legend of the Hummingbird," by Pura Belpre (from Puerto Rico). They will then be asked to write a legend of their own. They will share their story with a partner, and make any necessary changes in their writing. The students must either type or word process the final copy of their legend. They will share their legends with the class.
Associate: individual, pair-share
Subject: English
Intelligences: verbal/linguistic, interpersonal

6. Discuss with the class methods of structuring and documenting a research report. Place special emphasis on the following skills: gathering firsthand information, taking notes, paraphrasing, and creating a bibliography. Have students choose an article from a magazine to read. The article

may be relevant to either science or social studies. Ask them to take notes about the article, paraphrasing the most important information. Using their notes, they will write a summary of the article and an appropriate bibliographic entry for the article.
Associate: individual
Subjects: English, science, social studies
Intelligences: verbal/linguistic

7. Ask the students to bring their social studies report to class and their peers and instructor can make comments and give assistance on any necessary changes.
Associate: individual, small-group
Subjects: English, social studies
Intelligences: verbal/linguistic, interpersonal

Demonstrate

The reports, papers, and projects of this unit can become excellent demonstrations for portfolio assessment. Within each content area, the students can evaluate their achievements, utilizing the appropriate rubrics for each subject.

1. In science class, students will write a research paper about a disease. The paper will include symptoms and causes. An essential part of the paper will be to discuss not only how the disease they have chosen changes the body functions, but also how it affects an individual socially, emotionally, and intellectually. The English instructor will read and grade the papers for content, clarity, and correct language usage and mechanics.
Associate: individual
Subjects: English, science
Intelligences: verbal/linguistic, intrapersonal

2. In social studies, students will plan a Latin American culture fair. All projects from this unit will be displayed, including the students' social studies reports and legends from English class. Ethnic foods may be made available for tasting, and students may teach crafts or games. Prior to the event, let students know that the culture fair activities are the assessment for this unit.
Associate: small-group or whole-group
Subjects: social studies, English
Intelligences: verbal/linguistic, visual/spatial, bodily/kinesthetic, interpersonal, auditory/musical

Communicate

During the culture fair, student guides should explain to parents the theme of change in the three content areas. The students should specifically emphasize that the papers and legends were either written, revised, or evaluated in English class. It is important that the parents understand the purpose of the interconnectedness of discipline areas.

1. In science class, students will read their papers about the disease they have chosen to research to the class.
Associate: individual
Subjects: science, English
Intelligences: verbal/linguistic

2. In social studies, parents will be invited to the culture fair. Students will serve as guides or art/recreation instructors.

Associate: small-group or pair-share
Subjects: social studies, English
Intelligences: interpersonal

References

Arsenio Hall Communications. *Time Out: The Truth About HIV, AIDS, and You* (film). Hollywood, CA: Paramount Pictures, 1992.

Belpre, P. "The Legend of the Hummingbird." In *Literature Bronze* (pp. 621–624), E. Bowler et al, eds. Englewood Cliffs, NJ: Prentice Hall, 1994.

Bergman, C.A., and J.A. Senn. *Heath Grammar and Composition.* Lexington, MA: D.C. Heath & Company, 1987.

Beyer, B.K., J. Craven, M.A. McFarland, and W.J. Parker. *World Regions: The World Around Us.* New York: Macmillan/McGraw-Hill School Publishing Company, 1991.

Gray, B.G., et al. *World of Language.* Morristown, NJ: Silver Burdett & Ginn, Inc, 1990.

Mastervision. *Stages of Life: Reproduction, Growth, and Change.* New York: Mastervision, Inc., 1990.

Rand McNally. *Mexico* (film). San Ramon, CA: International Video Network, 1992.

Piggot, J. "Popocatepetl and Ixtaccihuatl." In *Literature Bronze* (pp. 613–620). E. Bowler et al, eds. Englewood Cliffs, NJ: Prentice Hall, 1994.

Platt, S. *Amazon, Land of Flooded Forest* (film). Washington, DC: National Geographic Society, 1989.

Prentice, M. *Catch Them Learning: A Handbook of Classroom Strategies.* Palatine, IL: IRI/Skylight Publishing, Inc., 1994.

WGBH Educational Foundation. *The Miracle of Life* (film). New York: Random House, Inc., 1986.

Wright, J., et al. *Exploring Life Science.* Englewood Cliffs, NJ: Prentice Hall, 1991.

Possibilities for Change

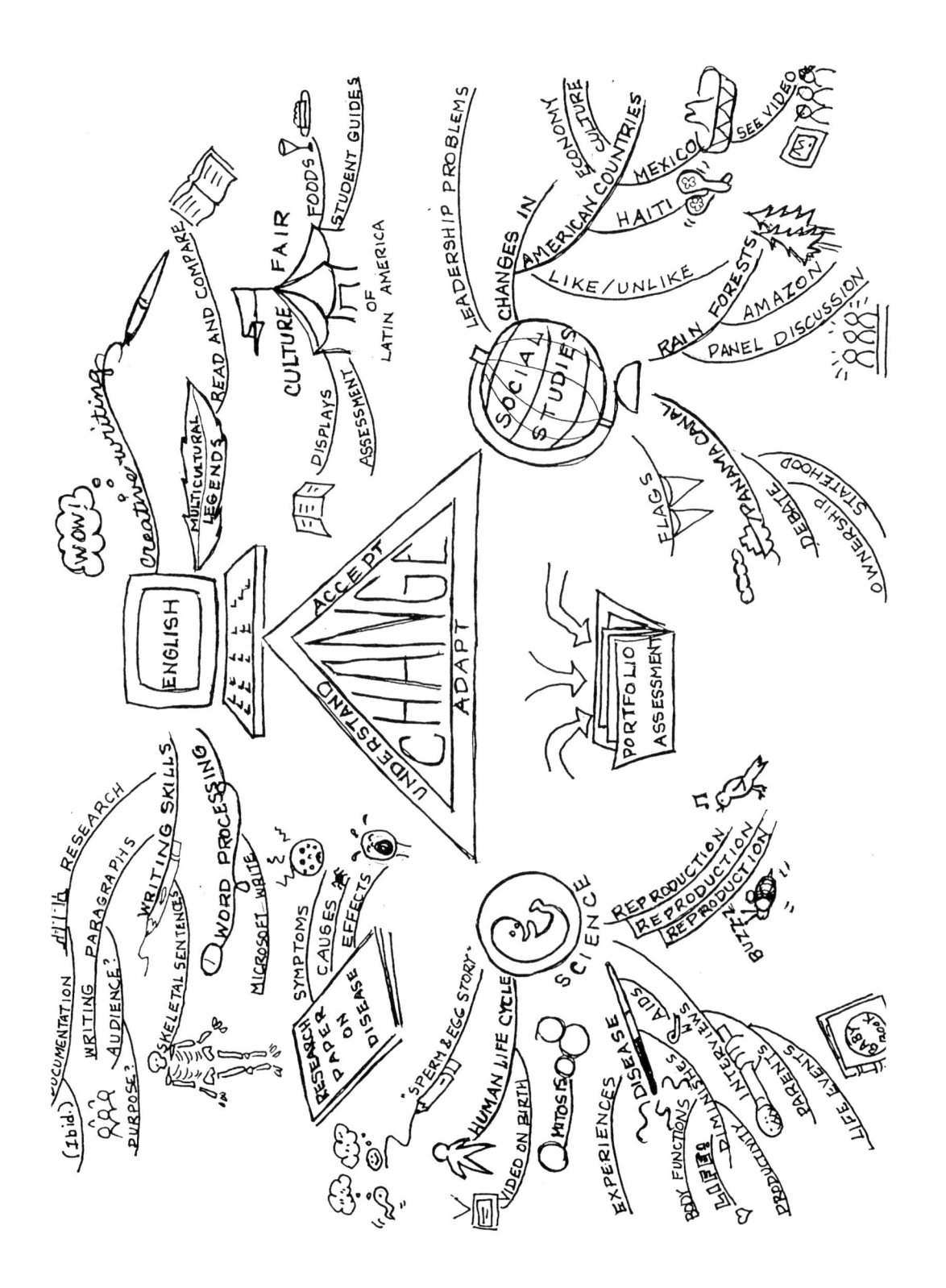

Social Studies Questions

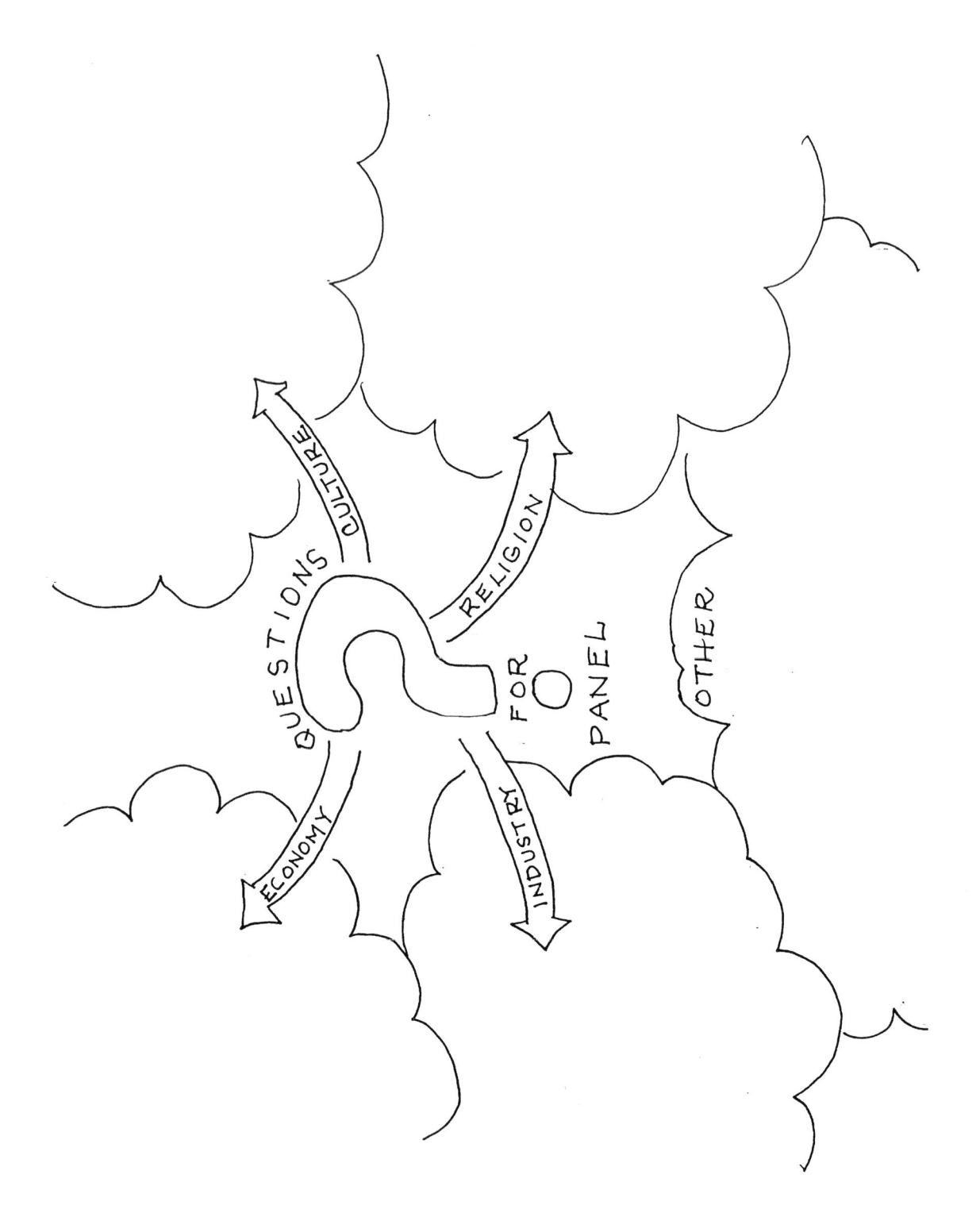

English Questions

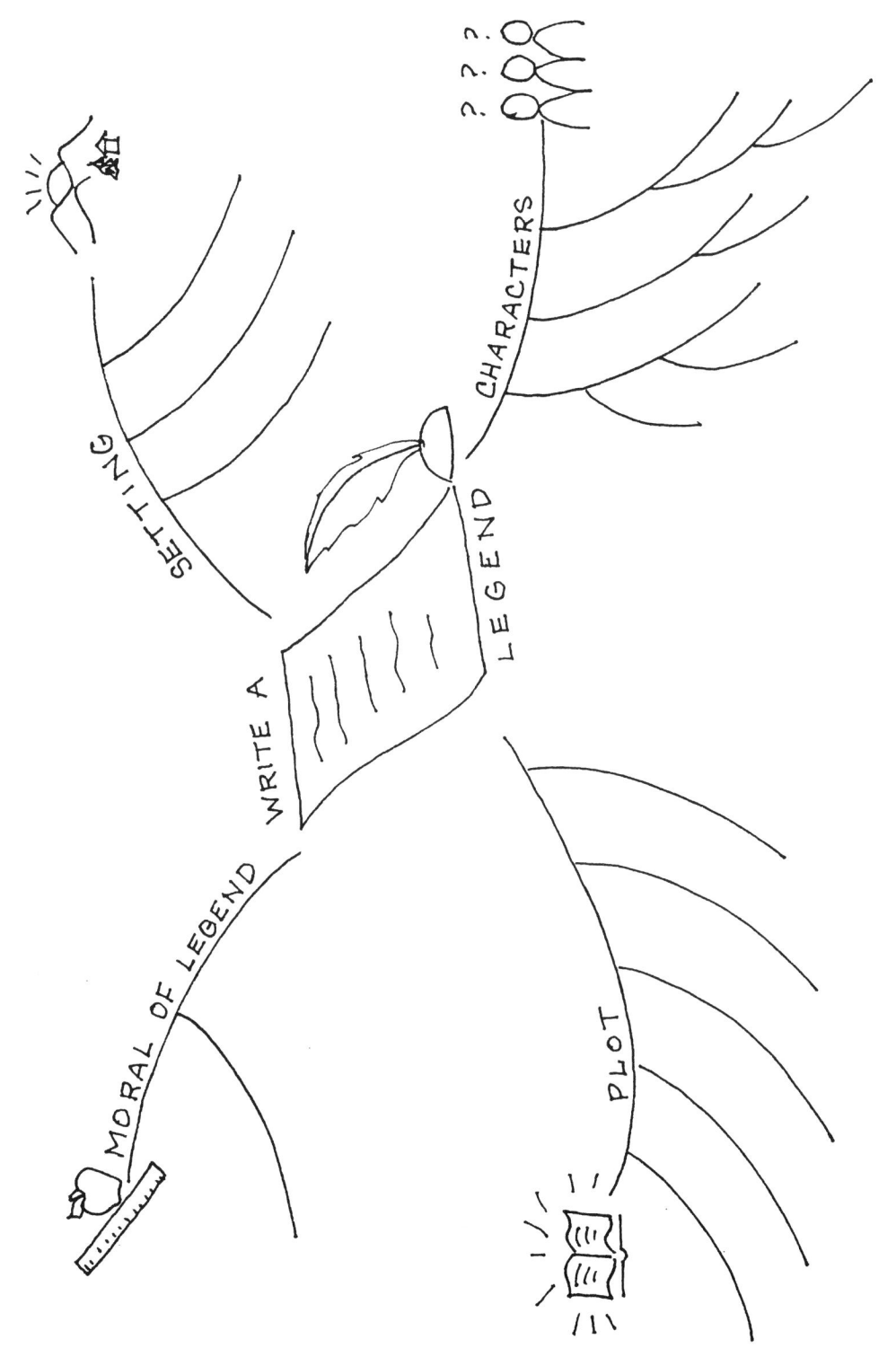

Write a Legend

- Setting
- Characters
- Plot
- Moral of Legend

Share Your Bright Ideas with Us!

J. WESTON WALCH PUBLISHER

We want to hear from you! Your valuable comments and suggestions will help us meet your current and future classroom needs.

Your name_____ Date_____

School name_____ Phone_____

School address_____

Grade level taught_____ Subject area(s) taught_____ Average class size_____

Where did you purchase this publication?_____

Was your salesperson knowledgeable about this product? Yes_____ No_____

What monies were used to purchase this product?

___School supplemental budget   ___Federal/state funding   ___Personal

Please "grade" this Walch publication according to the following criteria:

Quality of service you received when purchasing	A	B	C	D	F
Ease of use	A	B	C	D	F
Quality of content	A	B	C	D	F
Page layout	A	B	C	D	F
Organization of material	A	B	C	D	F
Suitability for grade level	A	B	C	D	F
Instructional value	A	B	C	D	F

COMMENTS:_____
_____

What specific supplemental materials would help you meet your current—or future—instructional needs?
_____

Have you used other Walch publications? If so, which ones?_____

May we use your comments in upcoming communications?   ___Yes   ___No

Please **FAX** this completed form to **207-772-3105**, or mail it to:

Product Development, J. Weston Walch, Publisher, P.O. Box 658, Portland, ME 04104-0658

We will send you a **FREE GIFT** as our way of thanking you for your feedback. **THANK YOU!**